THE
MADOFF
CHRONICLES

Inside the Secret World of
BERNIE and RUTH

Brian Ross

👑 | KINGSWELL

LOS ANGELES • NEW YORK

Copyright © October 2015 American Broadcasting Companies, Inc.

All rights reserved. Published by Kingswell, an imprint of Disney Book Group. No part of this book may be reproduced or transmitted in any form or by any means, electronic or mechanical, including photocopying, recording, or by any information storage and retrieval system, without written permission from the publisher.

For information address Kingswell,
1101 Flower Street, Glendale, California 91201.

Editorial Director: Wendy Lefkon
Executive Editor: Laura Hopper

Library of Congress Cataloging-in-Publication Data has been applied for.

ISBN 978-1-4847-5269-2

First Edition

Printed in the United States of America.

10 9 8 7 6 5 4 3 2 1

SUSTAINABLE FORESTRY INITIATIVE Certified Sourcing
www.sfiprogram.org
SFI-00993

THIS LABEL APPLIES TO TEXT STOCK

For Lucinda and Colin

CONTENTS

ACKNOWLEDGMENTS

Anyone who works in television news knows what a collaborative enterprise it is. The same is true of this book, my first.

I will be forever indebted to Ellen Archer, Will Balliett, Katherine Tasheff, Brendan Duffy, and Kristin Kiser of Hyperion for asking me to take on this project and its exciting electronic versions, which combine the printed word with the power of the visual. They treated this rookie with great kindness. Thanks also to David Lott, Shubhani Sarkar, and Vincent Stanley at Hyperion as well as Laura Hopper at Kingswell.

Ben Sherwood, James Goldston, David Westin, Kate O'Brian, and Kerry Smith, my bosses at ABC News, encouraged me throughout the process to expand the reach of our investigative unit and find new outlets for all we learned about the secret world of Bernie and Ruth. As always, I relied on the excellent advice and guidance of John Zucker and Betsy Schorr of ABC News, and my longtime friend Marty Lobel, even though they are lawyers.

My partner in digging through all of the court documents, tracking down witnesses, and confirming every last detail was the exceptionally diligent and talented Kate McCarthy of ABC News. No detail was too insignificant and no challenge too great as we learned together the joy of being able to write more than a minute-and-a-half report for *ABC World News with Charles Gibson*.

Since the night of Madoff's arrest, Richard Esposito helped ABC News "own" the story in his then-role as the network's senior investigative reporter. His connections and sources are without equal, and I will never forget how he gave up his seat in the jury box at Madoff's sentencing so I could get a close look at the man who had ruined so many lives yet still seemed more concerned about his wrinkled suit and unruly shirt collars.

Everyone at the ABC News investigative unit played an important role in our reporting on the Madoff scandal. Asa Eslocker, Joanna Jennings, Vic Walter, Nicholas Brennan, Yuliya Talanova, and Len Tepper spent many long days at work without complaint recording on video the life and times of Bernie and Ruth and their family and cohorts. Joel Stonington and Linsay Rousseau Burnett gladly accepted stakeout duty. Joe Rhee, Megan Chuchmach, Rehab el-Buri, Justin Rood, Ben Buchanan, and Maddy Sauer produced the broadcast and ABCNews .com reports that served as the basis for this book.

Avni Patel and Angela Hill worked tirelessly to learn

the stories of dozens of Madoff's victims and yet treat each one with the individual respect that was due them.

Anna Schechter's reporting from Palm Beach, Florida, provided extraordinary texture for the account of how Madoff so cavalierly swindled his fellow golfing partners and country club members. The Madoff inner circle was not happy to see her in town, but even after one of them smashed her camera, Anna kept digging.

Most important to me in reporting and writing this book is my longtime producer and friend Rhonda Schwartz, who now runs the ABC News investigative unit. Her tireless efforts and investigative coups are legendary in the television news business. Every chapter in this book is better because of her reporting. She rarely gets all the public credit she deserves for the award-winning investigative reports we have produced together for ABC News and NBC News, so it is a great pleasure to be able to thank her in print for so many years of partnership and excellence.

Finally, I need to express my great admiration and appreciation for the many people who spoke to me and my colleagues at ABC News about Bernie Madoff. Former FBI agent Brad Garrett provided invaluable insight into the workings of the criminal mind. Many of the sources of this book cannot be thanked by name because of the sensitivity of their positions.

Others took the risk, even when they were advised it

was not in their best interest to talk with me. Madoff's former secretary Eleanor Squillari, his former messenger "Little Rick," and his onetime security guard and confidant Nick Casale each provided a rare insight into the secret world of Bernie and Ruth and the largest financial crime in Wall Street history.

AUTHOR'S NOTE

The effects of Bernard Madoff's fraud were felt by thousands of people, and the news of his scheme's collapse was witnessed by many millions more. Thoroughly investigating such an epic crime is a challenge, and my team and I were tireless in interviewing investigators, victims, and many others. Countless hours were spent poring over court transcripts, video interviews, and SEC documents.

Authenticity is important to me, and I quoted directly from the original sources wherever possible. Some of this raw material is rough around the edges. In real life—unlike in the movies—villains aren't always articulate, victims aren't always able to muster eloquence in a moment of passion, and lawyers don't always get their tenses right. But this is an inside look into the world of the Madoffs—"you knows," "likes," and expletives included. The quotations included here might be ungrammatical in places, but they're true.

THE
MADOFF
CHRONICLES

ONE

The Arrest

"IKE, IT'S BERNIE."

The voice on the phone betrayed Bernard Madoff's Queens upbringing but sounded surprisingly young for a seventy-year-old man. And surprisingly calm, given the circumstances.

"I'm in the FBI office and I'm handcuffed to a chair," Madoff told his lawyer as he broke the news of his arrest for what would soon emerge as the biggest fraud scheme in Wall Street history.

Ira Lee Sorkin, a white-haired, veteran New York trial lawyer known as Ike, was visiting his granddaughter's nursery school in suburban Washington, D.C., when his cell phone rang. It was the afternoon of December 11, 2008.

A former prosecutor in the United States Attorney's Office in Manhattan and onetime head of the New York office of the Securities and Exchange Commission, (SEC), Sorkin was one of the city's premier criminal defense lawyers. He was as aggressive as they come and not easily caught off guard, but Madoff's call stunned him.

Madoff had called Sorkin ten days earlier and asked to meet with him about a "problem." According to Sorkin, they had been scheduled to meet on Wednesday, December 10, but Madoff canceled the meeting, pushing it back to December 15.

Instead of a day of legal strategy with his defense lawyer, Madoff had decided to set in motion a plan that would involve him confessing to his two sons, Mark and Andrew, and then letting them "do the right thing" and turn him in to the FBI.

He had asked his sons to give him a week to prepare, but events had moved much more quickly than he had planned. Two agents arrived at his Manhattan penthouse apartment at 133 E. 64th Street just before 8:30 a.m.— only twelve hours or so after his sons gave statements to federal prosecutors. Madoff, a meticulous, elegant dresser, was still in his pajamas, bathrobe, and slippers when special agents Ted Cacioppi and B. J. Kang of the FBI stepped off the elevator into apartment 12-A. They sat in his decorator-designed living room, and Cacioppi asked him if there was "an innocent explanation" for what his sons had described.

"No," said Madoff, who then calmly described what

he called a "fifty-billion-dollar fraud" that he said he had carried out by himself, with no help from anyone else. The agents told Madoff to get dressed, put him in handcuffs, and took him downtown to FBI headquarters at 26 Federal Plaza, where he was allowed to call his lawyer.

"Bernie, don't say another thing," Sorkin whispered to Madoff on the cell phone, trying not to disrupt the three-year-olds in the nursery school class, and unaware that his client, with no lawyer present, had already made a lengthy—if only partially truthful—confession to the FBI. From Sorkin's point of view, this was a legal disaster. He would never have advised Madoff to turn himself in and offer up a confession.

"If you have a client who robbed a bank, and there are video surveillance cameras and nine eyewitnesses, it might be a good idea to have your client turn himself in," Sorkin said. That was not the case with Madoff.

His monumental stock fraud had been carried out in great secrecy. Among the thousands of Madoff's victims were prominent New York financial figures, a number of Hollywood celebrities, some of the country's leading Jewish charities, and thousands of elderly retirees who had put their life savings in Madoff's hands because of his seemingly long and perfect track record of success. In some circles, he was called the "Jewish Warren Buffett."

It would turn out to be the biggest financial crime in the history of Wall Street, far eclipsing the 1980s insider trading scandals involving junk bond financiers Michael

Milken and Ivan Boesky. They were small-time operators compared to Madoff.

At the time of his arrest, Madoff's thousands of investors believed they had a total of $64.8 billion in accounts with him, even more than he had estimated to his lawyers and the FBI. The clients received monthly statements showing a series of trades in blue-chip stocks, and a reliable 12- to 20-percent rate of return, year after year, even in rough markets when everyone else was losing money.

It was all a lie. There were no trades. There were no double-digit returns. The money that came in from new clients was used to pay the existing clients their fabulous profits. It was a classic Ponzi scheme that would have made its namesake, Charles Ponzi, proud.

Ponzi was an Italian immigrant who became a multi-millionaire in Boston running a scheme from 1919 to 1920 that took about $15 million (about $160 million in today's value) from some forty thousand investors. Like Madoff, Ponzi promised impossibly high rates of return and had potential clients begging to invest. The scheme worked only as long as new money kept coming in so he could pay existing customers what he promised.

Ponzi's scheme collapsed in less than a year. Madoff's scheme ran for decades, fooling both government regulators and financial experts.

Until December 10, 2008, Madoff's fraud was still unknown to both the victims and the government, and given those circumstances, Sorkin could have had an advantage in fashioning a defense. He could have controlled when and how to come forward to the FBI and Department of Justice prosecutors and reveal what had happened. He might have been able to come up with an explanation for the missing billions that would have minimized Madoff's exposure to criminal prosecution.

"Maybe you say it was the bad market, maybe you say he lost his marbles," said one of the people briefed on the case. "Maybe you blame the evil government. You still need twelve people to vote to convict, and you really only need to persuade one to hold out. Maybe it takes a year or two, and then if you lose, you appeal, and the judge lets you stay in the apartment. That's three or four more years not in prison—that's a lot for someone his age."

But Madoff's arrest and confession scuttled any hope for that plan. He had his own plan.

"I'm running out of batteries. I'm going to call Dan. Don't say a word," Sorkin ordered Madoff as the lawyer used his remaining battery power in his cell phone to call his partner, Dan Horwitz, to get him down to the FBI office to stop his client from saying anything more.

As he turned back to his granddaughter's classroom, where the teacher was asking the students about the sounds made by barnyard animals, Sorkin was left to wonder why Madoff had turned himself in well before he had to, and without his lawyer's knowledge or presence.

Whatever it was that Sorkin might have been able to devise as a legal strategy, Madoff's last-minute decision set in motion a plan designed to protect the inner circle of those who were complicit in the scheme and, more important, shield his sons, his brother, and his wife, Ruth, from any suspicion. By claiming he "acted alone," Madoff saw himself as doing the "honorable thing" and taking all the blame.

Others familiar with the case suspected Madoff had made this dramatic move for a darker reason. They speculated that Madoff feared some of his more unsavory clients from Bogotá and Moscow would be very unhappy to learn their money had disappeared and would not hesitate to express their displeasure. Sonja Kohn, a Vienna-based operative for Madoff who had brought in a number of wealthy European investors, was said by investigators to have gone into hiding "from very angry bears." Being under arrest by the FBI was certainly better than being targeted by the Russian mob.

Whatever his motives, people who were around Madoff in those few days after the arrest say he seemed quite pleased with himself. Even in the face of what would have been a devastating series of events for anyone, Madoff maintained the cool, aloof demeanor for which he was well known. He was still on his game.

"The con artist is always going to go for the very last con because that is the nature of their antisocial personality," said former FBI agent and veteran crime profiler Brad Garrett, now an ABC News consultant. Garrett, who profiled and cracked the cases of some of the country's most elusive criminals during his career at the FBI, said Madoff is a classic case of the antisocial personality, someone completely self-absorbed, with no conscience. "'What's in it for me?' they will ask. 'Is it in my interest to tell you the truth, or to tell you enough of the truth to get you off my back?'"

By confessing to such a grand scheme, Madoff had caught the FBI and prosecutors completely off guard.

"Antisocial personalities are control freaks," explained Garrett. "And in his mind, getting in front of the FBI was the best thing for him. I think he believed, 'If I admit the shell of what we've been doing and I take all the blame, A, I won't get a superlong sentence and B, no one else will be charged.'"

Within days, Madoff came to believe his plan was working. Prosecutors, desperate for his help in unraveling the enormous scheme, had gone along with Sorkin's request that Madoff not be locked up. They even made concessions when Madoff had trouble meeting the conditions of the $10 million bail imposed by a federal magistrate.

Madoff and his wife, Ruth, easily met the financial conditions by posting their $7.5 million New York apartment and additional cash as collateral for the bond. The judge, however, had also required four "financially responsible persons" to cosign for Madoff. He could find only two: his wife and his brother, Peter. So the government compromised and allowed Madoff to stay free with only two cosigners as long as he stayed in the apartment, obeyed a 7 p.m. to 9 a.m. curfew, wore an electronic monitoring device on his ankle, and arranged for Ruth to surrender her passport. He had already surrendered his.

Many of Madoff's former customers, his victims, were outraged. They were facing bankruptcy and foreclosure on their homes because of his crime, and he was allowed to await trial in one of the city's finest apartment buildings, whose other residents included Matt Lauer, the cohost of the NBC News *Today* program.

After decades of conning investors and SEC regulators, Madoff thought he had successfully conned federal prosecutors. He believed he could "sell" his version of events and manipulate the agents and prosecutors, who would need months to figure out what Madoff had been doing. He thought "he would be out of prison in time to watch the grandchildren grow up," according to one person who heard what he said after his arrest.

After all, Michael Milken had served only twenty-two months in prison for what, until December 11, had been considered one of the biggest Wall Street criminal schemes. Madoff seemed certain that "there will be a life after this."

Prosecutors later admitted to associates that they had been conned by Madoff. "We lost round one, but we don't plan to lose any others," one of the prosecutors said.

As smug as Madoff might have been about his ability to deceive the FBI, having his sons turn him in was hardly his ideal scenario. Indeed, his decision to orchestrate his arrest came after a whirlwind three weeks during which he finally concluded that his life of privilege and wealth could not be saved.

As the world's financial system began to collapse in the fall of 2008, with Lehman Brothers and other long-established firms facing disaster, Madoff recognized that the same tsunami would be heading toward him.

His Ponzi scheme had survived previous economic downturns because, in general, his investors, his "marks," were convinced that Madoff represented a safe haven. Like most legitimate hedge funds, he put no restrictions on the ability of investors to withdraw their money at the end of each year. But given the steady 12- to 20-percent returns Madoff had been able to achieve with what were known as his "don't ask" trading strategies, few investors wanted to pull their money out of their accounts with him.

Many suspected that Bernie might have been cutting a few regulatory corners, but investors felt that the monthly statements from Bernard L. Madoff Investment Securities LLC "don't lie." His investors had stuck with him through the market corrections of the 1980s and 1990s, and even through the precipitous crash of stock prices that followed the 9/11 attacks of 2001.

But the fall of 2008 was different. Not since the Great Depression had there been such doubts about the stability of the world's economy. Banks were being shut down to prevent runs that many feared could create a domino effect across the country. Consumer confidence was at a record low. Many of Madoff's biggest investors needed to pull some of their money out of the safe haven to shore up losses elsewhere. A few were even starting to question whether he was a fraud. How can he still be doing so well when everybody else is not? What do we know about his secret strategy anyway? Suddenly, Madoff needed $7 billion and he had nowhere near that amount.

His firm's account at JPMorgan Chase, #140081703, had dropped to near zero several times during the fall, and in the end it had only $234 million on deposit. The amount in the account was his cushion, his only cushion, and it was Madoff's daily obsession.

Wherever he was—even on vacation in Palm Beach, the Hamptons, Mexico, or France—Madoff would get a report at the end of every day about the Pow in and out of the Chase account.

"He would call in around five thirty, and I would always have to have the reports for him," recalled his longtime secretary, Eleanor Squillari.

"There were just two columns of numbers, with names next to them," she said. "One would have a plus in front of it, and the other would have a minus. Bernie had to know those numbers at the end of every day." Investigators believe what she saw was the daily cash in/cash out report of his JPMorgan Chase account.

Another set of figures "had to be filed in chronological order in a very specific place in his office," said Eleanor. "I didn't read that to him." Investigators think those reports were the daily computer runs of closing stock prices that Madoff would consult when he created the fictional trades.

The reports were prepared under the direction of Frank DiPascali, who had managed to become Madoff's chief financial officer despite his lack of a college education or any background in finance. With his pronounced Queens accent and gold chains, DiPascali struck some former employees as being like a character out of *Goodfellas*, Martin Scorsese's movie about low-level mafia figures and wannabes. DiPascali was one of the few employees, investigators determined, who knew the full nature of the Ponzi scheme, and was deeply involved in carrying it out. He ultimately made a deal with the government and agreed to testify against his former colleagues in court. He died in May, 2015 of lung cancer, a few months before he was to be sentenced to prison.

"I never got a feel for him as a financial genius," recalled former employee Bob McMahon, who was hired to help maintain and improve the computer system at the Madoff office. "The first time I saw him, I thought he was an electrician or running cable."

Madoff did not need a financial genius. He did not need to know whether the market was up or down, or even whether the firm had made money in trades on any particular day. There were no actual trades, only the fictional transactions. Madoff never made any investments for his clients all those years. Anyone visiting the Madoff offices would have wondered how that could be possible given the hectic activity on the nineteenth-floor trading room. All of the employees on that floor worked for another part of the Madoff business that was legitimate and made trades for large institutional customers. The investment advisory business was completely separate and completely crooked. All that really mattered for that part of the business was the cash flow in and out of the Chase account. All withdrawals had to come out of that account. As with any Ponzi scheme, the scam could continue only as long as more money came in than went out.

Between 2006 and 2008, records showed that the Chase account had an "average balance of several billion dollars." But by mid-November 2008 the daily balance had dropped close to zero on a regular basis. Madoff ordered his London office to sell its holdings in British treasury notes and transfer at least $164 million to the Chase account. Customers had taken out $320 million in November, and only $300 million had come in. Madoff realized there wasn't nearly enough coming in to cover what his longtime clients would want to take out by the end of the year. Madoff needed $7 billion by the end of the quarter.

So he scrambled to perpetuate the scam by trying to recruit new clients and secure more deposits from current clients. People in the office noticed he seemed preoccupied, but few knew why.

"All these heavy hitters were coming in," his secretary, Eleanor, remembers. "I'm saying to myself, Bernie must be doing really well, and he must be under a lot of pressure and that explains why he hasn't been himself."

She would learn a few weeks later just how badly she had misjudged the cause of her boss's anxiety.

In the days before Thanksgiving, Madoff's appointment book shows he met on November 25 with Ezra Merkin, a New York financier and close friend who had $2.4 billion of his clients' money with Bernard L. Madoff Investment Securities. Much of the money Merkin sent to Madoff came from Jewish organizations, including Yeshiva University, where Merkin served on the board of trustees.

Merkin declined to speak about the meeting with Madoff other than to say, through a public relations spokesperson, that he too had been fooled by "the intricate, fraudulent scheme perpetrated by Madoff."

On that same day just before Thanksgiving, Madoff's wife, Ruth, came into the office and withdrew $5.5 million from an account she had with Cohmad, one of the companies co-owned by her husband, which recruited investors for Bernard L. Madoff Investment Securities. The money was wired to another account. Ruth was preparing for something.

She had been by Madoff's side for fifty years and would remain loyal even after the arrest. She had kept the books in the early days in the 1960s and continued to balance the checking account in an office one floor below Bernie's that she still had on the day he was arrested.

On Thanksgiving Day itself, Madoff came into the office. "That had to be big," said Eleanor, who could not recall Madoff ever working on any holiday.

"Do you want me to come in, too?" she asked him. "No, no, no need," Madoff replied. Then he asked her where the coffee was kept in case his visitors wanted something.

The appointment book, turned over to the FBI and provided to the author by Madoff's secretary, shows he met with representatives of Optimal, the asset management side of the huge Spanish bank Santander.

It's not known if the Spanish bankers were being asked for more money or demanding to pull their money out, but the bank later reported it lost almost $2 billion invested with Madoff on behalf of its clients. A spokesperson for the bank refused to comment on the meeting. Unlike other large funds, Bank Santander originally said it would reimburse its clients for their losses. The bank later agreed to a $235 million settlement with the Madoff trustee.

After the meeting, Madoff flew to Palm Beach for the rest of weekend, during which he would mark his forty-ninth wedding anniversary.

In the first week of December, Madoff confided to one of his sons that he "was struggling" to raise the necessary funds to cover withdrawals but "thought that he would be able to do so," according to an FBI affidavit. This was a very big red flag for the Madoff sons, who were, at best, bliss-fully ignorant of their father's scheme until the very end.

Many of his longtime investors said they were "too stretched" to put any more in, but ninety-five-year-old Carl Shapiro agreed to help out. Shapiro, who became a multimillionaire in the garment industry, had been one of Madoff's first "millionaire" investors and had trusted Madoff with his money for forty years. Madoff used Shapiro's son-in-law, Robert Jaffe, to recruit more customers, and earlier in 2008, Madoff had attended Shapiro's ninety-fifth birthday party in Palm Beach.

Shapiro already had about $295 million in accounts with Madoff, and now he agreed to invest $250 million more. People familiar with Shapiro's dealings say Madoff promised "nice, above average returns" for an investment of only a few months.

Now, with Shapiro's money, essentially a short-term loan, Madoff had managed to get his cash account balance at Chase back into the black. He had just scraped by with a huge redemption payout on November 19, but he was still far short of the $7 billion he needed for all the other withdrawals clients had requested. If the checks did not go out, everyone would know Madoff was a fraud.

Two weeks later, Shapiro would learn that the entire $545 million he had entrusted to Madoff was gone.

As the days went by, Madoff was still Mr. Cool to the outside world, and only a few of those close to him saw the tension building. Madoff's blood pressure shot up,

Eleanor remembered. "He was taking blood pressure medicine and his back was killing him," she said. "He was walking crooked and we tried to give him a pain patch. He could make it through meetings with investors, but then he would collapse afterward. I'd see him lying on the floor," she said. "His eyes would be closed and his arms outstretched, like a dead person."

Eleanor says her boss never confided in her about what was really going on, but she is convinced he had pretty much given up by early December.

"At one point, out of nowhere, he told me that he was sorry he had been so hard on me," she remembered. "He never said anything like that before. Then he started throwing the mail back at me, saying he didn't want it," she said. "He was so preoccupied, his voice was very low and I kind of felt like I was working by myself."

Still, Madoff tried to keep up outward appearances.

On Monday, December 8, three days before he would be arrested, Madoff hosted a meeting of the board of the Gift of Life Bone Marrow Foundation, which raises money to help Jewish victims of leukemia and lymphoma find bone marrow transplant donors. His nephew, Roger, died of leukemia in 2006, and his youngest son, Andrew, was diagnosed with lymphoma in 2003.

Madoff was chairman of the board of the charity and had served on the board along with a who's who of other wealthy Jewish New Yorkers, including Merkin and real estate developer Fred Wilpon, the owner of the New

York Mets baseball team. Many of the board members were also investors with Madoff, including Wilpon, who reportedly lost "hundreds of millions of dollars." (The Mets were later forced to announce they still had enough money to meet the team payroll, despite the losses attributed to Madoff.)

As the board members gathered that Monday evening in Madoff's nineteenth-floor conference room, Madoff already knew he would be out of business by the end of the week. People in the room—many longtime friends—would soon learn he had willfully cheated them without batting an eye that night or ever.

"If you don't have a conscience, then that is not a problem for you," said former FBI agent Garrett. "I call them hollow people because on the outside they can smile, they can be charming, they can be engaging, and on the inside there is nothing. They have no emotions. They couldn't care less about you. He's thinking, 'I did these people a favor and I'm just going to continue to act as I normally act: smile, shake their hand,' knowing in a few days he might be in jail."

A notice on the Gift of Life Bone Marrow Foundation's Web site says its funds were "not managed by Madoff" but that the losses suffered by many of its contributors "understandably impacted" their charitable giving.

His secretary said Madoff "was his normal self that night" at the charity board meeting.

The next day, Tuesday, December 9, Madoff canceled

the meeting scheduled later in the week with his lawyer, Sorkin. He also canceled a meeting scheduled that day with investment banker Ira Harris and his son Jonathan Harris, according to Squillari, his secretary. They would not talk about their relationship with Madoff, but the secretary said the senior Harris had been meeting regularly with Madoff and appeared to be "giving some advice," but she did not know the subject of the advice. The canceled meeting was to take place in a New York hotel.

There were no meetings on Madoff's calendar for Wednesday, December 10.

Instead, around 10:30 a.m., he asked his two sons, Andy and Mark, and his brother, Peter, to come to his office on the nineteenth floor.

An hour or so earlier, Ruth had again come to the office to withdraw more money from her Cohmad account. She ordered $10 million wired to another account. With the pre-Thanksgiving withdrawal of $5.5 million, Ruth and Bernie now had a $15.5 million stockpile set aside for what was about to happen.

Eleanor knew something unusual was happening when Ruth came in. "She was up to something. I remember turning around and seeing her scoot by me and she just started with this nervous laugh."

Then Eleanor saw the two sons arrive. They appeared to have been summoned to their father's office.

"I thought there was something wrong with the family," she recalled. The marriage Madoff's youngest son, Andy, had been on the rocks for some time and he already had a girlfriend, Catherine, whom he had brought around to the office. Some thought she was his fiancée, even though he was still married. His wife, Deborah, would file for divorce the next day, the day her father-in-law was arrested.

The family gathering in Bernard Madoff's office, however, was not about the divorce.

Madoff's younger brother, Peter, arrived first. Bernie had told Peter about the scam and the coming collapse the night before, according to a person on one of the Madoff family legal teams. Then Mark and Andy came in. Mark had been told the night before by his father that he was going to distribute all the cash in the checking account as employee bonuses, normally paid in February, because "he had recently made profits through business operations, and that now was a good time to distribute it." Mark knew something was wrong, he later told the FBI, and called his younger brother, Andy, who was less involved with the business on a day-to-day basis. "We have to meet with Dad," Mark told Andy.

Mark and Andy told the FBI that when they challenged their father about the payments, he said he wanted to move the discussion to his apartment, because he "wasn't sure he would be able to hold it together" if they stayed in the office.

After a few minutes, Bernie was through talking. Eleanor says she saw the sons get their father's overcoat, help him on with it, and then walk out of the office.

"Where are you going?" Eleanor asked.

"I'm going out," he said, with the collar on his dark green cashmere coat turned up, shielding his face.

"We're going Christmas shopping," Mark told the secretary.

Eleanor didn't believe it. "I knew something was wrong. They seemed to be pretty anxious, they were in a rush."

Peter stayed behind, giving no indication for the rest of the day that there was any problem.

The two boys and their father climbed into one of the firm's black Cadillacs for the quick trip to Madoff's apartment about twelve blocks away. "They mostly talked about the grandchildren," recalled the driver. "Mark sat in front, and Andrew and his father sat in back."

It was unusual for the three of them to be leaving the office in the middle of the day, and the driver said he sensed something wasn't right.

The sons told the FBI that when they got to their father's apartment, he quickly confessed he was a fraud. "It's all just one big lie," he reportedly said, calling it "basically a giant Ponzi scheme." "I'm finished," he told his boys. "I have absolutely nothing."

After being told by their father that his life had been a lie, that he was a crook and a cheat, Mark and Andy left the apartment and told the driver they were going to get lunch before heading back to the office. But Mark and Andy never returned to the office. Mark and Andy told the FBI that their father asked them to keep quiet about the scam for a week while he "wound up" his affairs. Then, he expected them to contact authorities so they would be the heroes, turning in their own father. At least, that was Madoff's plan.

Instead, his sons immediately called a lawyer, Martin London, the stepfather of Mark's wife, Stephanie. London, now retired from the firm Paul, Weiss, is a famed litigator who represented Vice President Spiro Agnew in the bribery case that led to his resignation in 1973. London himself was an investor with Madoff. Realizing the enormity of the problem, London sent the Madoff boys to another lawyer in his firm, Martin Flumenbaum. By 4 p.m. that afternoon, Mark and Andy were in Flumenbaum's law office and by 5:30 p.m. they were giving statements to federal prosecutors and the SEC.

An hour after telling his sons, one of Madoff's drivers took Madoff back to the office and listened in as the boss talked to someone on his cell phone.

"Don't worry; everything is going to be okay," Madoff said to the person on the other end of the call, describing the progress of his plan to have his sons turn him in. "Of course, they were scared shitless," Madoff said into the phone.

Eleanor says she was told the phone call was to Frank DiPascali, and that Madoff told DiPascali that his son Andy "pissed his pants" when his father confessed his crimes.

The driver says he took Madoff back to the building,

but he never showed up in his actual office on the nineteenth floor, according to Eleanor. She would not have seen him if he had gone directly to the firm's seventeenth floor, where the Ponzi scheme was run and where files and incriminating documents were kept.

Remarkably, hours later Madoff would host the firm's holiday party at Rosa Mexicano, an upscale Mexican restaurant on Manhattan's East Side, famous for its pink pomegranate frozen margaritas. The yearly holiday party was eagerly anticipated by his employees, who always dressed up for the occasion. Sometimes Madoff would come in black tie and Ruth would wear her latest designer dress. On this night, he came in his office outfit, a dark suit.

Madoff and Ruth, and Peter and his wife, Marion, attended and, according to employees present, gave no indication that in twelve hours everyone's life would be changed, and not for the better.

Ruth sat down next to one employee and asked what he was going to do for the holidays. "We're going to Florida," Ruth told the employee.

The only thing that seemed strange to some employees was the absence of Madoff's two sons. They did not attend the party. They were busy meeting with lawyers, prosecutors, and the FBI, arranging for their father's arrest the next morning.

TWO

The Early Days

EVEN AS HER HUSBAND SAT IN JAIL IN DISGRACE WHILE HE awaited his sentence, Ruth Madoff remained loyal to the man who had swept her away on a New York City beach more than fifty years earlier.

She told one family member that there never had been and never would be another man in her life.

Their love story continued as she dutifully visited Bernie on Mondays at a federal prison, enduring the social humiliation of her weekly visits and braving the endless barrage of questions from reporters seeking to find out what she knew about her husband's systematically cheating investors out of an estimated $65 billion.

"I'm not talking to *you*," she indignantly told one reporter from ABC News as she tried to flag a cab outside the Metropolitan Correctional Center in Lower Manhattan after a visit. She could no longer afford the sleek black sedans and drivers that once took her wherever she ordered.

Like Bonnie and Clyde, Bernie stole for a living and Ruth had enjoyed the ride. Historians are still divided on what role Bonnie Parker played in Clyde Barrow's Depression-era bank robberies across the Midwest, but there was no doubt she loved him deeply.

Like Bonnie, Ruth followed her man no matter where he went. And it had been a long and wondrous ride. The Madoffs enjoyed the kind of luxury and privilege that had been unimaginable to them as they grew up in a middle class, mostly Jewish neighborhood in Queens—the children of parents with their own shady connections.

The two met as teenagers. Ruth remembers Bernie as handsome and suntanned, sitting in the lifeguard chair in his swimsuit at the Rockaway Beach where, according to the New York Department of Parks & Recreation, he worked three summers as a lifeguard.

He was three years older than Ruth.

At five foot one, Ruth was "a beautiful little blond girl," said former classmate Diana Goldberg. Friends remember Ruth as vivacious and affable. Another classmate, Richard Cohen, a *Washington Post* columnist, recalled her as "really cute, an object of desire across a classroom or another." Bernie was almost six feet tall and had a wiry, athletic physique. As a member of the high school swim team, the Mermen, he swam the butterfly or breaststroke on the medley team. According to his senior yearbook, Bernie was also one of the athletes who served as a locker room guard. The locker guards saw themselves as "tough guys" who would "play chicken" by slamming their fists into each other until one gave up because of the pain. Bernie told friends he thought it was a "dumb" game but endured the bruised knuckles because he could not let the "idiots" think he was chicken.

Life for two teenagers in love in Laurelton, the section of Queens where they lived, resembled something out of *Happy Days*. After the movies on Friday nights at a theater known as "the Itch," the Laurelton crowd would head to Raab's ice-cream parlor to gossip and flirt. Once they got their driver's licenses, Bernie and his friends would venture out to Peninsula Boulevard to go bowling at Falcaro's. Bernie and his best friend, Elliott, formed a social club called the Ravens and wore sweaters emblazoned with a Raven patch, remembers Jay Portnoy, a childhood friend and fellow Ravens member.

While technically in New York City, Laurelton was far from the gritty urban center. The tree-lined streets were a place of single-family houses, where Dad went to work in Manhattan and Mom stayed home. Life revolved around the children and school and temple, although neither Ruth nor Bernie was remembered as being very religious.

The Madoffs lived in a two-story brick house with a small backyard at 139-54 228th Street. Bernie was a member of Boy Scout Troop 225, which met at the Jewish Center in Laurelton. As a scout, Madoff would regularly raise his right hand and take the oath "to help other people at all times; to keep myself physically strong, mentally awake, and morally straight." He did manage to keep physically strong and mentally awake after he left the scouts, but not much else.

Bernie's parents, Sylvia and Ralph, had lived on Manhattan's Lower East Side when he was born. After the birth of a second son, Peter, and then a daughter, Sondra, they sought the suburban dream and moved out to Laurelton. The Madoffs quickly made themselves at home in their new neighborhood.

Bernie played on an intramural basketball team, where he was known for "stealing the ball," said former classmate Michael Yessner. "No one could steal the ball like Bernie."

Ruth was considered very bright—much smarter than Bernie, who was, at best, a B+ student. "Definitely above average, but not of the genius caliber," said Portnoy of Madoff. But Bernie was remembered as being cagey in school, able to use a glib tongue to get ahead.

"He hadn't read a book and he was called on in English class to give a book report," remembers Portnoy from their sophomore year. "So Bernie got up there and just made it up while he went along. After Bernie's presentation, the teacher looked a little suspicious. She asked Bernie to show the class the book, but Bernie said he had already returned it to the public library."

Madoff would be just as good at fudging fifty years later, in 2006, when the SEC began to investigate allegations he was running a Ponzi scheme. He talked his way out of trouble by creating a fictional set of books for the investigators, making it all up just as he had in his sophomore English class. Even though the investigators knew Madoff had somehow "mislead" (sic) them, they eventually closed the case, reporting they could not find "evidence of fraud." His high school English teacher had done no better at exposing Bernie's classroom scam.

Bernie went off to college at the University of Alabama in the fall of 1956. One of Bernie's friends said he claimed he had won a swimming scholarship at Alabama; however, school records show Alabama did not have a varsity swimming team until several years later and that there were "no swimming scholarships" at the time. While he was away at college, Ruth, still a junior in high school, remained loyal and wrote him long love letters.

He wasn't in Tuscaloosa long. He made an effort to fit in there by joining Sigma Alpha Mu, founded as "a fraternity of Jewish men," but Alabama was an unlikely college choice for a city kid from New York. In the same year Madoff was there, the school's first African-American student was accepted and then expelled three days later "for her own safety" after a student mob threatened violence.

After only three months in Alabama, Madoff returned to New York and was back in the arms of Ruth. He enrolled at Hofstra College in January 1957, and other than a few months in training at Fort Bragg during his three years of service as a second lieutenant in the Army Reserves, Bernie and Ruth would be together, almost every day, for five decades, until he was put behind bars on March 12, 2009.

She still found him sexy at age seventy.

Despite the false start in Alabama, Madoff moved through Hofstra without a hitch, graduating in 1960 with a BA in political science. Madoff commuted from his home, about ten miles away, and he's not remembered as having had much of a presence on campus. There's no mention or photo of him in his graduating class yearbook. Years later, in 2004, Madoff's presumed financial genius earned him a seat on the Hofstra board of trustees. He was still a member of the board on the day of his arrest. Fortunately for Hofstra, it has a strict policy of not doing business or placing its endowment with any member of its board of trustees.

During college Bernie earned about $5,000 running a business with his brother, Peter, installing irrigation pipes for suburban homeowners who wanted perfect green lawns. That was a lot of money in 1960, but Madoff's intention was to pursue a career trading stocks. America was in a boom, and while there was money to be made servicing suburban lawns, Madoff knew he could make a lot more as an investment broker than as a landscaper.

Peter told Bernie's secretary, Eleanor Squillari, that Bernie ran the business and would use Peter "to go and collect bills, collect the monies, because Peter was cute and charming."

In early 1960, Madoff took the test that brokers are required to pass before being licensed to trade stocks and securities. Within a month of graduation, Madoff had passed the general securities representative test and had founded Bernard L. Madoff Investment Securities. He tried law school but dropped out after only a year at Brooklyn Law School. Madoff started by trading penny stocks in over-the-counter markets and that business would, over the decades, grow to become a huge and legitimate trading operation that dealt with large institutional customers and was well known on Wall Street.

Less well known was Madoff's investment advisory business, which served as the foundation of his Ponzi scheme. The corporate structure for Madoff's life of crime had been established.

His decision to join the financial industry may well have been influenced by his parents and Ruth's parents.

Ralph and Sylvia Madoff ran a suspect investment company out of their house under the names Gibraltar Securities and Second Gibraltar Corp. of Laurelton, New York. These businesses were registered in Sylvia's name only. Some reports say Ralph had "tax problems" and didn't want his name publicly attached.

In 1963, the SEC moved to revoke the broker-dealer license of the Sylvia Madoff companies, for "alleged failure to file financial reports," according to an SEC announcement from September 1963. Four months later, in January 1964, Sylvia Madoff withdrew her SEC registration and shut down the businesses, which had the effect of stopping a full investigation from being launched. The decision to close up shop may have been motivated by her instinct to protect her son—much in the same way Bernie himself sought to protect his inner circle when he saw the end coming.

By the time his parents had come under suspicion at the SEC, Bernie Madoff's securities trading operation was already up and running—and already crooked, according to what Madoff said to a person he confided in after his arrest. This person insisted on anonymity because of the sensitivity of the ongoing investigation, but Madoff said, "It began almost immediately and for the first few years, there were a lot of sleepless nights. But then I realized I could do it." A scam from day one.

This account is corroborated by an investigator, who was tasked to "reconstruct" Madoff's fraud but not authorized to speak publicly. The investigator says the available evidence shows that the scam was well in place at least by 1964 or 1965, and "likely back to the beginning or near the beginning," when Bernard L. Madoff Investment Securities first opened its doors.

If true, this calls into question Madoff's statement

under oath when he pleaded guilty in March before U.S. District Court judge Denny Chin. "To the best of my recollection, my fraud began in the early 1990s," Madoff told the court. It was the only key fact in his plea allocution prefaced with the "best of my recollection" hedge.

Federal prosecutor Marc O. Litt immediately challenged Madoff. "The government does not entirely agree with all of the defendant's description of his conduct," said Litt to Judge Chin. "The defendant operated a massive Ponzi scheme through his company, Bernard L. Madoff Investment Securities, beginning at least as early as the 1980s." Prosecutors are still trying to figure out precisely when it started, but it was certainly long before the date Madoff told the judge.

This is a significant detail. If that statement was a lie, or if Madoff's "recollection" was not at its "best" that day, and the scam did begin in the 1960s, it would also call into question the role of Ruth and many other Madoff family members and employees who were with Bernie in the early days. His brother, Peter, joined the family business in 1967. Ruth was there from the beginning.

Ruth and Bernie were married in 1959 at the Laurelton Jewish Center, two years before she graduated college. Ruth breezed to a degree in psychology from Queens College in three years, eager to begin life with Bernie. Once she was finished with school, Ruth helped to keep the books at Bernie's company. At that time, Bernard L. Madoff Investment Securities was still a shoestring operation. Peter was fond of telling the story of how Ruth and his brother first ran the business from a folding card table in their apartment.

As important as Ruth was to business operations, Ruth's father, Saul Alpern, was even more essential. Alpern was a New York accountant who began to steer money to Madoff's company from customers he knew in Queens or met while playing bridge over hot water and lemon at summer resorts in the Catskills. Hundreds of frugal retirees ultimately lost their savings because of following Saul's recommendation from decades earlier.

"Our place was fertile territory," recalled David Arenson, whose family ran the Sunny Oaks resort in the Catskills where Saul Alpern and his wife, Sara, would spend the summers. Having heard Saul's account of his son-in-law's ability to pick stocks and earn big returns year after year, the retirees were eager to get in. "The fund only required about five thousand dollars to get in, so it wasn't like you had to be rich. And they were promising something like eighteen to twenty percent."

The investors were grateful to be included by Saul in the great opportunity that Bernie's investment company represented. When Bernie and Ruth would visit Ruth's parents at Sunny Oaks, it was all very cozy. "In Yiddish, they'd say it was *haimish*, which means down-home and folksy," said Arenson. "There was an element of trust."

It was a family affair. Ruth kept the books, her father brought in the money, and Bernie pulled the strings, quickly becoming well known for his uncanny ability to make money even when others were suffering in down markets. Ruth loved her father and saw a lot of Bernie in him. "He really has such a great mind," Jay Portnoy recalls Ruth saying of her father. "Don't you think my father looks so brilliant?"

As brilliant as his daughter thought he was, Saul Alpern's dealings with Bernie would later lead to big trouble for his accounting firm, Alpern & Heller, which began recruiting clients for Madoff in 1962. By 1992 his firm had funneled $441 million into Madoff's hands.

Alpern's accounting office was located in Manhattan, on East Fortieth Street between Fifth and Madison avenues. Among Alpern's employees were two accountants named Frank Avellino and Michael Bienes, who would later become partners when Heller died. When Alpern retired in 1974, the company dropped his name and became Avellino & Bienes. Even after Alpern's departure, the firm continued to feed millions of dollars to Madoff for investment. According to SEC documents and people who were involved at the time, many of Avellino & Bienes's clients had no idea of Madoff's role in the business. The accountants guaranteed rates of return between 13.5 and 20 percent, the same impossibly high rates of return that Madoff had offered throughout his career to investors who could be considered gullible or greedy or both.

Frank Avellino and Michael Bienes made a fortune feeding money to Madoff. Bienes had homes in Fort

Lauderdale, Florida, and London, where he was considered an American bon vivant and major contributor to the Royal Opera House. Avellino had homes in New York, Nantucket, and Palm Beach.

In 1992 the SEC finally became suspicious and opened an investigation of Avellino & Bienes, but took no action against Madoff, even though investigators learned he was involved. At the time, he had already served two terms as chairman of the NASDAQ exchange. It would be the first of at least eight times the SEC and other federal regulators launched investigations of Madoff or his associates but failed to uncover his scheme.

According to a person involved with the firm at the time, SEC investigators were looking into allegations that Avellino & Bienes were involved in a Ponzi scheme. The investigators discovered that Madoff was handling the investments for Avellino & Bienes, but they did not or would not connect the dots that would have exposed Madoff's role as the true master of the scheme. As proof that everything was legitimate, Madoff offered to return all of the money that had been invested by Avellino & Bienes. Investigators say that the records that would prove whether he did return the money are still being sought.

In a civil enforcement complaint, the SEC said that between 1962 and 1992 Avellino & Bienes had guaranteed customers "interest rates ranging between 13.5% and 20%" by investing with "one broker-dealer" who was not named. The unnamed "broker-dealer," of course, was

Madoff. In 2009, investigators began going through SEC archives to determine just why Madoff's name was not included.

The SEC imposed $350,000 in fines against Avellino, Bienes, and their firm for failing to register as securities dealers, but no criminal action was taken against them. The lawyer representing Avellino and Bienes in 1992 was Ike Sorkin, the same lawyer who would represent Madoff sixteen years later. Asked whether he was suspicious of Madoff at the time, Sorkin said he could not talk about it. "We took the position that he returned all of the money," said Sorkin.

According to Madoff's secretary, Eleanor, Avellino and Bienes continued to be in occasional contact with Madoff. She said Madoff ordered her to always refer to them as "A and B but never by their actual names" if they called.

When Madoff's scheme collapsed in 2008, Michael Bienes lost much of his fortune and was forced to give up his apartment in London and sell his home in Fort Lauderdale, according to his lawyer, Mark Raymond. There was "never any indication that this was a Ponzi scheme," said Raymond. "If they had known," he added, "Michael would not have lost millions and would not be millions in debt." The lawyer said Bienes had very little contact with Madoff after 1992 and had not seen him in person since the funeral of Ruth's father in 1999. With his money gone, Bienes moved to a small apartment in Fort Lauderdale.

A lawyer for Frank Avellino had no comment.

A second set of accountants was also charged civilly by the SEC in 1992 with illegally funneling clients' money to Madoff without being properly registered or licensed. They were Steven Mendelow and Edward Glantz, principals of Telfran Associates, who were also represented by Ike Sorkin.

Mendelow and Glantz shared offices with the original Alpern firm on East Fortieth Street in the 1960s. They were not allowed to invest directly with Madoff but had to steer all of their customers' money through Alpern, Avellino, and Bienes.

Even after Mendelow and Glantz were cited and fined by the SEC, they continued as well to have ties to Madoff. Mendelow was already working for the accounting firm that handled some of Madoff's government filings, and his private number was found in Madoff's "little black book" of what his secretary said were his essential contacts.

Glantz died in 2005, and Mendelow insisted he had met or spoken with Madoff only a half dozen times since being introduced to him in the early 1990s. He said he can remember Madoff calling him only once in the fifteen years they knew each other.

The *Wall Street Journal* described the action against the four accountants in 1992 as a crackdown on "one of the largest-ever sales of unregistered securities." Yet there was no mention of Madoff in the SEC documents, and he would continue to operate for sixteen more years—expanding the list of his victims and the breadth of his scheme every year.

With Madoff left unscathed by the SEC investigation, there was no rush for investors to pull their money out in 1992. In fact, the elderly investors at Sunny Oaks, and others recruited by Ruth's father, were told there was nothing to worry about and that they could deal directly with Madoff. The minimum investment was soon raised to $50,000. Every month, or every quarter, David Arenson recalls, he and others would receive impressive-looking statements that showed steady growth based on a series of trades involving blue-chip corporations. Of course, the trades never took place. It was all a lie.

It was a lie that David Arenson feared could cost him his life. He was diagnosed in 2003 with chronic lymphocytic leukemia. "I'm going to need a bone marrow transplant. And the money that I had in Madoff, and that my family had in Madoff, would've gone a long way toward making that doable," he said. Arenson died March 6, 2014.

Arenson and the summer residents of Sunny Oaks were among the early Madoff "marks"—in the parlance of con men—and some of the least wealthy. Many of them had first put their money with him when Madoff was still building his scam, years before the steady stream of multimillionaires and mega-millionaires would trust Madoff with their wealth. By targeting retirees, Madoff established a client base unlikely to pull its money out. They were happy with the steady returns Madoff promised and delivered. When someone died, the account was usually rolled over to the children. As long as most of the "marks" didn't want to cash out, the scam could roll right along.

If anything, the fact that Madoff had been untouched by the SEC actions against Avellino & Bienes and Telfran Associates only served to authenticate and burnish his credentials.

The 1992 article in the *Wall Street Journal* dismissed speculation that Madoff had done anything suspect.

"Who was the broker with the Midas touch?" the article asked. "None other than Bernard L. Madoff—a highly successful and controversial figure on Wall Street, but until now not known as an ace money manger."

Interviewed by the *Wall Street Journal*, Madoff gave a long, technical description of his "Midas touch" strategy. He said he was able to hedge against the market's ups and downs with futures and options and boasted of his "stock picking." Sixteen years later, he would tell a federal judge that that same strategy was a fraud, just the false cover for his Ponzi scheme. But at the time the article was written, it was very reassuring for Madoff's investors to read.

"That further added to the luster that we were dealing with someone who knew what he was doing, and was legitimate," recalled Arenson. "There certainly wasn't any idea that anything was wrong."

A year later, in 1993, Madoff was elected to a third term as the chairman of NASDAQ.

Overlooked by the SEC and lauded by the *Wall Street Journal*, Madoff enjoyed the golden life as an industry titan, untouched by regulators and courted by wealthy investors.

While Ruth's father had been the first of many who would feed millions of dollars into Madoff's criminal enterprise, he was never publicly implicated in his son-in-law's scheme. He did not become superrich, as many of the subsequent "feeders" to Madoff would. When Ruth's mother, Sara, died in 1996, her will indicated she had about $2 million in three Madoff accounts, half of which ultimately went to her daughters, Ruth and Joan.

When Ruth's father, Saul, died three years later in December 1999, he left the two daughters only 992 shares of Pitney Bowes stock and $39,000. Thanks to Bernie's "success," Ruth was so well off at the time that she gave her sister all of the stock.

After her husband's arrest, Ruth's lawyers tried to argue that she was entitled to keep at least $62 million in assets that she had "inherited" from her parents. Investigators quickly dug out the Alpern wills to dispute that contention.

Despite speculation that Ruth may have had a role in her husband's financial scam, the government found no evidence to support she was a knowing accomplice in the Ponzi scheme and she was not prosecuted.

Former FBI agent Brad Garrett says such Bonnie-and-Clyde couples have their own dynamic. "Did Bernie ever really tell Ruth what was really going on? Maybe a little bit, but probably not to any great extent, because he didn't need to. She probably didn't care at the end of the day.

"People with antisocial behavior like Bernie pick partners who are dips, people who are unaware, just want to live the life that somebody like Bernie has created," said Garrett. "They'll just deny what is going on around them." The early years had been difficult as Madoff ironed out the kinks in his scheme and learned how to keep beyond the reach of federal regulators. But he learned that they were easier to fool than his high school English teacher. And fool them he did.

When it finally all came tumbling down, only Ruth's love was left.

THREE

House Arrest

THE MAÎTRE D' HEARD SCREAMS, THEN SOBBING.

It was late afternoon on Thursday, December 11, and lunch in the main dining room of the Palm Beach Country Club came to an abrupt halt. Bridge games were abandoned, meals were forgotten.

The news of Bernard Madoff's arrest had begun to spread among his thousands of investors. There had not yet been any public announcement from the FBI, and the news had not yet hit the wires or cable TV, but whispered phone conversations that began from inside Madoff's New York offices quickly spread the story to Wall Street, across the country, and around the world. The whispers turned to cries of disbelief and then to shouts of anger and then tears born of fear.

The members of the Palm Beach Country Club were in a panic. Bernie and Ruth were prominent members of the club. It had been considered a sign of status to be "accepted" by Bernie as an investor. They had entrusted their fortunes to him and now he was under arrest for securities fraud.

At Madoff's office, the phone lines were jammed as investors tried to find out what had happened.

Eleanor Squillari had come into the office around 7 a.m. that morning. She liked to be in early to get a jump on the day and organize her boss's daily calendar. His schedule for this day appeared to be completely free.

At 7:30, there was a strange phone call from Ruth about her sons, Mark and Andy. Eleanor says that Ruth asked her "if I saw the boys yet. And the hairs on my neck went up. She can call them on their portables, but she asked me."

Mark and Andy had not attended the previous evening's office Christmas party, and that had also struck Eleanor as strange. She had no idea that Mark and Andy had gone to the FBI to turn in their father.

Now their mother seemed desperate to know where they were. Eleanor looked into the trading room on the nineteenth floor where Mark and Andy normally were stationed by 7:30 a.m. She told Ruth she didn't see them.

"And then I heard her say to who I think was Bernie,

'They're not there.' I knew something was wrong," Eleanor recalled.

A short time later, Eleanor went down one flight to see her friend Jean, the receptionist on the eighteenth floor, the firm's main entrance. The nineteenth floor was the location of Bernie's office and the seventeenth floor that was the legitimate arm of the business. The seventeenth floor was the center of the Ponzi scheme in a room with highly restricted access.

She saw Bernie's brother, Peter, in the conference room with men she did not recognize. "What's he doing here?" she wondered. "Because Peter never gets in that early."

Jean told her, "They're lawyers."

"And then a man comes storming in," Eleanor recalled. "He's in a trench coat and he flashed his badge, typical FBI look." It was Ted Cacioppi, the agent who would arrest Madoff half an hour later.

"I went running to Peter, who never looked up. And one of the men just said, 'We're expecting him.'"

Eleanor returned to the nineteenth floor. "I just sat at my desk, knowing something horrible was happening. I thought it was an extortion, I thought it was kidnapping." As the morning went on, Annette Bongiorno called Eleanor "an unusual amount of times" looking to talk to Bernie. She was one of the people regarded by investigators as part of the inner circle that carried out the criminal scheme. She seemed desperate to find Madoff.

Eleanor placed several calls to her boss on his cell phone, but there was no answer. She did not know that he was already in handcuffs, placed under arrest by the FBI.

She finally found out what was happening when Peter's secretary, Elaine, overheard her boss talking.

"Peter's telling people that Bernie was arrested for securities fraud," Elaine reported.

"I was like, no, it can't be, it just can't be. What are you talking about?" Eleanor said.

Peter looked like a defeated man. "Peter did not seem surprised," Eleanor recalled. "The shoulders slumping, he just looked beat. I saw Peter at his worst after this happened and he was just a basket case."

Peter had seemed fragile to people in his office since the death of his son, Roger, from leukemia in 2006. Now his brother was under arrest, and he was left in charge to explain the situation, even while he must have been pondering his own fate. Peter was the firm's compliance officer, and his daughter, Shana, was a compliance lawyer for the firm. Their job was to make sure that all business conducted at the family firm was legitimate. Many firms prohibit the family members of top executives from serving as compliance officers because of possible conflicts of interest, but not Madoff. Peter spent hours in his office that day sobbing, with his head in his hands.

Annette arrived on the nineteenth floor, still looking for Bernie after all her phone calls.

"I told her to go see Peter," Eleanor remembered. After

a brief conversation with Peter, Annette "made a beeline for the elevator, never looked at me. I never spoke to her again. She just left. That was it."

For Eleanor, Annette's reaction spoke volumes. "How do you not be in shock and say, 'What the hell is going on?' I'd known her for twenty-five years. How do you just walk right past me and leave?" It was a reaction that would make sense if you're afraid you might be the next one to be arrested.

Then Madoff's other right-hand person on the seventeenth floor, Frank DiPascali, arrived outside the executive offices. Madoff had apparently spent much of the previous afternoon on the seventeenth floor with DiPascali, in one of two rooms marked DO NOT ENTER and DO NOT CLEAN.

DiPascali's reaction to the news was different, but just as strange as Annette's, according to Eleanor. "His hands were shaking and he walked up to Peter. He goes, 'Uh, so what's going on?' And Peter said, 'Bernie was arrested for securities fraud.' And he went, 'Oh, yeah?' and turned around and left. Just nothing seemed right. But then, nothing was right."

DiPascali returned to the seventeenth floor, the operational headquarters of the scheme, where the documents and incriminating files were kept. The phones were already ringing off the hook, but he ordered that "no one answer," according to a former employee. Later he and Annette prepared a "script" for seventeenth-floor employees to use in dealing with worried clients. Soon, most other employees left, and for the remainder of the day of the arrest, and early on the next day, Friday, DiPascali would be free to do whatever he wanted on the seventeenth floor. According to a former employee, the FBI had sealed off the premises and shut down the computers by Friday morning and all employees "were herded to the eighteenth floor."

As the day went on, the volume of phone calls from distraught clients overwhelmed Eleanor, Elaine, and others trying to help. "And we were all taking turns because you would get sick after fifteen minutes," Eleanor remembered.

As they called in, seeking reassurance that the news was wrong, that their money was safe, Eleanor did not know what to say. She still believed there had been some "paperwork mistake" and that everything would be sorted out. She couldn't reach Madoff and finally decided to ask DiPascali. He was by himself on the seventeenth floor talking on his cell phone.

"Frank, what are we gonna do? What am I supposed to be telling people?" she asked.

He looked at her for a moment and then said, "Tell them nobody's available," and went back to his cell phone conversation.

Calls were coming in from around the world. One of the first calls was from Jeff Tucker, whose investment firm, Fairfield Greenwich, had steered billions of dollars of its clients' money to Madoff. On the day of the arrest, Fairfield Greenwich clients thought they had $7.2 billion invested with Madoff.

Some friends called to support Madoff. James Davin of Davin Capital Corp. sent a fax addressed to Ruth and Bernie. "If there is *anything* we can do to be of help, it will be done." It was signed, "Jim and Tina."

By early evening, the initial, sketchy reports about the arrest were beginning to show up. The *Wall Street Journal* published its first report about Madoff's arrest at 4:25 p.m.

At Elaine's, the legendary Manhattan restaurant and club, then ABC News reporter Rich Esposito stared at his BlackBerry. There was little that happened in the criminal world that wasn't known to Esposito and the other reporters, cops, private investigators, and defense lawyers who were part of the regular crowd. There was no talk yet about the Madoff case and the owner, Elaine Kaufman, who knew almost anyone worth knowing in the city, had never even heard of Madoff. Nor had Esposito, a veteran police beat reporter, until a cryptic message from the FBI came through on his BlackBerry announcing Madoff's arrest in a $50 billion investment scam.

"Must be a typo," said one of Esposito's colleagues. "Maybe they forgot the decimal point. Must be $5 billion, couldn't be $50 billion."

Esposito sent a message back to get the real figure.

No, the reply came, $50 billion was correct. The man under arrest had given the FBI the number himself. And he was the former chairman of the NASDAQ exchange.

"If all that's true," said Esposito, "it would be the biggest financial scam ever. Ever."

It was well into the evening, but Esposito and reporters all over New York were beginning to scramble.

Later that Thursday night, ninety-five-year-old Carl Shapiro was at home in Palm Beach, in his luxury condominium next to The Breakers hotel, when his son-in-law, Robert Jaffe, called and told him to turn on CNN. Shapiro had just given Madoff $250 million in cash for what was to be a "nice, short-term investment" to help Bernie through the financial crisis.

The news about Madoff from Anderson Cooper was not reassuring. He was speaking over "Just In" news footage of Carl's old friend Bernie coming out of the federal courthouse in New York City in a driving rain.

"Some late news, very strange and troubling news out of Wall Street tonight. Former NASDAQ stock exchange chairman, Bernard Madoff, out on a ten-million-dollar bond tonight; there he is. He was charged today with securities fraud," said Cooper.

It got worse.

"The federal complaint accusing him of conning clients in his investment firm out of billions of dollars; what's more, the complaint alleges that yesterday Mr.

Madoff told senior employees that the company was, quote, all just one big lie. And, quote, basically, a giant Ponzi scheme. No immediate comment from him or his attorneys."

By Friday morning, it was clear that Bernie Madoff was under arrest for a lot more than some vague "securities fraud" or paperwork problem. This was no "failure to file SEC reports" or "failure to register."

There were no more calls and faxes in support of Madoff at his office. It was getting ugly, and Eleanor Squillari was now starting to have doubts about her boss of twenty years.

She was in early again from her home on Staten Island, and the first call came from Ruth Madoff. Ruth said she urgently needed the PIN number of her husband's cell phone so she could divert the phone bills from the office to the apartment. The company would not change the billing address without the PIN number. Eleanor immediately knew that Ruth and Bernie were up to something.

"Bernie lived by his phone. He always had to have his phone," she recalled. In fact, even when he was in the office, he would use the cell phone for the most sensitive calls. Now he wanted to make sure the bill and records of who he had been talking to over the last month came to him at his apartment.

"I didn't know the PIN number, and the person who did know the PIN had just lost their entire fortune," Eleanor noted. She couldn't bring herself to call the employee, Amy Joel, for the PIN number even though Ruth was pushing hard. "And Ruth called again, and again, and she was very insistent about getting the PIN number. This was a big deal for her."

Eleanor was getting a bad feeling. She had tried to be optimistic. She had tried to deny the growing doubts. She still didn't believe what was being said about Bernie on television. She did not realize the truth until she finally talked with Madoff later that Friday. It was a conversation she still could not recount without breaking down in tears.

"How are you? How's Ruth?" was the first thing she asked him. "It was a very short conversation. I didn't know what to say." She did not ask him if the allegations were true. "At that point I didn't believe it and I just felt so horrible for them, and scared."

Madoff talked in a low voice, but seemed to be eerily calm. "He even called me 'sweetie,' which he never does."

But then as he began to speak, the pieces started to fall together for Eleanor.

"He didn't say, 'Eleanor, how are you? What's going on with the clients? Eleanor, we're gonna straighten this out,'" she said.

Instead, Madoff was solely concerned with what the FBI had found in his office.

"All he said was, 'Anybody been in my office? Have

they gone in my briefcase? Have they gone in my diary?' That's all he wanted to know. That was it."

Now Eleanor was in tears. She knew her boss and knew what he had done. The briefcase he always took with him was missing. It was a black leather file case with a long handle and wheels, like the kind used by lawyers and pilots. Bernie kept files on the accounts and the "feeder funds" in the case and traveled with it everywhere. In its place that morning, said Eleanor, was a vinyl substitute that looked like, but was not, the original. Other items left in his office seemed conspicuous by their presence.

"He planted things for them to find," she said. Eleanor said Madoff was pleased to hear that the agents had gone through his office and his desk.

Among the discoveries were signed checks for $173 million that Madoff had made out for employees and certain investors. His secretary is convinced that Madoff never intended to send them out and that he just wanted them to be discovered so it would reflect well on him. Madoff told someone later that he wanted "to take care of the poor bastards" who he knew would soon be unemployed. Madoff's lawyers told the FBI where to find the checks in Madoff's desk.

"It was all just part of the setup. He had to convince his sons that he was having a nervous breakdown or that something was not right and he was gonna do a good thing.

I think he wanted to look better. He needed sympathy, he needed everyone to say, okay, he was gonna try to take care of them.

"I told the FBI, if he's trying to convince anybody that he's losing it, come and talk to me because I know he was [as] calm a cucumber up until the day of the arrest," she said. "He is so good, we know now, at manipulating everybody. In the entire world."

It was during that brief phone conversation that Eleanor says she came to believe her boss was a crook. She is no expert, but her perspective about her boss's behavior is remarkably similar to the analysis by former FBI agent Brad Garrett.

"If you are as egocentric as people like Mr. Madoff are, then you're going to think you can control the court and control the prosecutors and control the whole situation by getting out in front of them and starting to manipulate," explained Garrett.

Madoff remained in control, reading the morning papers and watching the news at his nearby penthouse apartment. His visitors over the next few weeks saw "absolutely no sign of emotion" from Madoff. "He was just somebody who had stepped back from his inner soul," said Nick Casale, a former New York City police detective whose firm was hired to provide security for Madoff and make sure he lived up to the terms of his bail. "He was almost blank, he didn't show emotion. A serial killer type." Madoff methodically made a list of the school and charity boards from which he would now have to resign.

He continued to enjoy his favorite cigars from Davidoff and spent his evenings at his computer or watching old movies with Ruth in one of two dens in the duplex apartment. Madoff and his wife were accustomed to walking around at night naked but they had to adjust once Casale's firm installed surveillance cameras in the apartment. The arrest was barely mentioned in Casale's presence and Ruth tried her best to act normally. "I never saw her get angry with him," said Casale. "She was not only losing her husband to prison, but she was losing her status in the community and her wealth and her position, her lifestyle."

As he waited for his lawyers and federal prosecutors to negotiate a plea deal, Madoff remained an arrogant, aloof, heartless man who, to many, seemed to actually take pride in this monumental fraud that had fooled so many on Wall Street. "He did not seem like the most contrite person I ever met," said Casale, who spent hours with Madoff in the apartment. There was no sense of shame. Bernie might have come from the outer borough of Queens, but he had played with the big boys in Manhattan.

"One of the key points with him is that he wanted to be king of the mountain. That's extremely important to people with antisocial personality problems because it's a control, it's an ego thing," said former FBI agent Garrett.

Similarly, Ruth didn't seem to be affected by the extraordinary amount of pain Bernie had caused so many people. Instead, she spoke with disdain of "the gentiles" she felt were enjoying her husband's downfall. She complained to another member of the family that the courts freezing the Madoff family assets on behalf of the victims were unfair because the judges were elected and had a bias for their constituents.

Some legal system, Ruth said, as if she and Bernie were the aggrieved victims.

At the same time, Ruth asked Bernie's secretary, Eleanor, to help her pay a bill for the family yacht, the $7 million *Bull*, moored at Cap d'Antibes on the French Riviera. Ruth told Eleanor the authorities and the bankruptcy trustees "don't have to know about this," Eleanor recalled. She ignored Ruth's request.

"I just went to the FBI and I said, I think they're trying to escape. I told them about the boat thing. I just didn't get back to her," Eleanor recalled. She was through being conned by the Madoffs.

While they didn't talk much about the people Bernie had hurt, the Madoffs did seem obsessed about the photographers waiting outside their apartment. Until he pleaded guilty, the only apology issued by Bernie Madoff was a note to other residents in the Sixty-fourth Street apartment building, regretting the disruption caused by the photographers, reporters, and satellite trucks that surrounded the building. Bernie thought that people who had paid $5 million to $10 million for an apartment certainly shouldn't have to put up with that.

Dear neighbors,

Please accept my profound apologies for the terrible inconvenience that I have caused over the past weeks. Ruth and I appreciate the support we have received.

Best regards,

BERNARD MADOFF

His investors never received any such written apology from Madoff.

He ignored all requests for interviews, including one hand-delivered by the doorman from fellow building resident Matt Lauer.

And Madoff went to great lengths to dodge photographers as he went to and from court, peppering Casale and his security team with thoughts on how to get a van with black windows to block the photographers, "and then they can't snap my picture in the car," and also "discouraging them from blocking the entrance to the building."

His house arrest had been part of Madoff's plan as he had orchestrated his confession to his sons back in December. At first, prosecutors thought Madoff would be a fully cooperating witness who would help them understand what happened to the money. To the outrage of his victims, the government did not object to him being released on bond. He was required to pay for twenty-four-hour coverage by Casale's private security firm.

On Christmas Eve, at about 5:30 p.m., right after Casale and the court-ordered security guards had left the apartment, Bernie and Ruth had another trick up their sleeves: Ruth went to a nearby post office jammed with last-minute holiday business. Paying in cash, she mailed five large white envelopes, uninsured, with no return address, to the Madoffs' two sons, Andy and Mark; Madoff's brother, Peter; Madoff's sister-in-law; and one to old friends. Inside the envelopes were some of the family's precious jewelry, bought and paid for with money stolen from clients. One package contained thirteen watches, one diamond necklace, an emerald ring, and two sets of cuff links, altogether valued at approximately $1 million.

Bernie enclosed a note to his sons.

> Dear Mark and Andy,
>
>   If you can bear to keep these watches, they are given with my love. If not, give them to someone who might.
>
>   Love, Dad.

When their sons received the jewelry and the note, they called their lawyers, who called the FBI.

Ruth and Bernie maintained they were just sending "sentimental personal items" as gifts. Investigators and agents took a different view. Prosecutors began to realize they, like so many others, had made a mistake trusting Madoff. It appeared that the Madoffs had violated court orders and were trying to furtively distribute some of their wealth into the hands of relatives before the victims or the government could get it.

But there was another theory. Some investigators believe they sent the jewelry to the sons so they could turn it in and further establish their credentials as the "good guys" in the scandal, not at all in league with their father. One veteran investigator likened it to how a spy who knew he had been compromised would arrange for another spy in his cell to turn him in to deflect attention.

A federal magistrate accepted Madoff's innocent version of events—that it was just some small trinkets, personal items. The magistrate concluded that Madoff had not acted to hide his wealth, and that his sons had done the right thing by reporting the episode to the FBI. Prosecutors got nowhere when they attempted to cite the Christmas Eve mailings as proof that Madoff should be locked up.

Prosecutors had already begun to realize that Madoff had no plan to cooperate fully. After the first "confession" in December, Madoff was never again permitted by his lawyers to speak with FBI agents. He was sticking to his story that he did it "alone," which, given the enormity and complexity of the fraud scheme, the FBI was discovering could not possibly be true.

"He gave the FBI a sack of shit," said one investigator familiar with Madoff's apparent strategy. "It was Bernie saying, 'I stole fifty billion dollars, now you can go figure out what you want to do.' This will take years to unravel."

When prosecutors moved to have Madoff jailed, his lawyers arranged for Casale's security firm to come up with a plan to persuade the judge Madoff could be kept safely guarded under house arrest at his apartment.

Casale was paid $250,000 by Madoff for his efforts, with the prosecutors' approval. Casale reported directly to Madoff's lawyer, Ira Sorkin, and Madoff himself. It was a huge conflict of interest that even Casale acknowledged. He said that "if Bernie took off, I would certainly make a phone call, but it would not have been my job to tackle him on the street."

Given that prosecutors say that all of Madoff's money was stolen from his clients, this meant that his clients were, essentially, paying for the guards so Madoff could avoid jail and stay in his $7.5 million penthouse, which also was paid for with their money.

FOUR

The Office

FOR THE MOST PART, BERNIE MADOFF LEARNED TO LIVE with being a criminal.

Still, there were times when the tension built and he worried, not so much about the victims, but about getting caught and losing the life of wealth and privilege he had built for his family.

So when it was time to party, Madoff seemed eager to blow off steam. On those occasions, especially in the early days, a messenger known in the office as Little Rick would be dispatched to Harlem to bring back marijuana for Bernie and others in the office.

"No executive from Wall Street wanted to go up to Spanish Harlem. They're not gonna go to a hole-in-the-wall and get a little envelope and put money in it," recalled Little Rick, a short, muscular man with a Puerto Rican Flag tattooed on his left bicep. "I was the messenger. That was my job."

A grateful Madoff gave Little Rick the title of manager.

"Little Rick knew everyone, and knew everything. Whenever anything shady had to be done, Bernie had Little Rick do it," recalled one Madoff employee.

Little Rick said that Ruth Madoff was also appreciative of his drug runs. He recalled fondly how Ruth would sometimes share her grass with a friend going through chemotherapy. "She was a wonder, always trying to help somebody."

Other former employees have told investigators that Ruth was at one point a "heavy user" who would sometimes blame her faulty memory on the grass she smoked.

Little Rick ended up losing his job in 2003 when he couldn't kick his own problem with cocaine and drugs were discovered in his desk. He says he wasn't the only one with a problem at the Madoff firm. "There was white powder all over that office. It was like the freaking North Pole," Little Rick said. "Are you freaking kidding me?"

Little Rick said Bernie and younger brother Peter called him in to let him go. "Rick, why did you get yourself to this point? You know we tried to get you help," he recalls Bernie saying.

"I know," said Little Rick, looking straight at Bernie. "You tried to push me to go to rehab a long time ago. But the same person who pushed me to go to rehab is still doing drugs. Bernie, maybe I was conditioned."

Little Rick said Peter immediately got up. "What are you talking about? What are you trying to say?" he recalled Peter shouting, attempting to defend Bernie's honor.

"Peter, shut the fuck up and sit down, now," he recalls Bernie yelling.

"He sat down and put his tail between his legs, because Peter did not bump heads with Bernie even after all these years. When Bernie told you sit down and shut the fuck up, that's what you did."

Little Rick says Bernie wanted the separation to be as friendly as possible.

"I cried when I left there. He cried. He hugged me."

It was rare for Madoff to fire anyone. There were far too many secrets to be protected. Whatever illegal activities Little Rick was guilty of paled in comparison to the massive criminality his boss was engaged in on a daily basis.

The Madoff offices were located on three floors of an architecturally distinguished building known as the Lipstick Building, on Manhattan's Third Avenue, at Fifty-third Street. With its oval shape and three red-granite layers stacked on top of one another, set off by stainless steel horizontal bands, the thirty-four-story building resembles an extended lipstick tube. Madoff's close friend and client Fred Wilpon was one of the developers, and Madoff was among the first tenants when he signed a lease in 1986.

Madoff had come a long way from the folding table in his Queens apartment. One of his first real offices had been in space he shared with an old friend, Marty Joel, at 39 Broadway, near the New York Stock Exchange. (Madoff delivered the eulogy at Joel's funeral and he hired Joel's daughter, Amy, to work for him. The Joel family thought it had more than $20 million invested with Madoff, and was wiped out when their loyal friend and Amy's boss was revealed to be a crook.)

As the firm grew, Madoff moved to larger quarters at 110 Wall Street, where Little Rick recalls wild times in the 1970s and 1980s.

"At one Christmas party, Bernie rented out the entire floor of the disco New York New York, and there were topless waitresses and waiters in just G-strings," said Little Rick. "That was before spouses came to the parties."

Office flings were "part of the scene," and Little Rick said some of the employees took delight in using Bernie's or Peter's office to have sex late at night. Little Rick said they especially liked using Peter's office, because he "could be such a hard-ass.

"Peter was always complaining about how dirty his sofa was and having it cleaned. It was a thrill to do it there," he said.

The offices at 110 Wall Street soon became too small for Madoff's grand ambitions. As the money from investors rolled in and the millions of dollars turned to hundreds of millions and then billions, Madoff's prestige grew and his ego demanded an office that reflected his position.

"The owner's name is on the door," boasted Madoff in promotional material posted on the company's Web site. "Customers know that Bernard Madoff has a personal interest in maintaining the unblemished record of value, fair-dealing, and high ethical standards that has always been the firm's hallmark," stated the profile Madoff published about himself. The profile said Madoff founded the firm "soon after leaving law school." It did not specify that he had dropped out of law school after one year.

The Web site went on to describe how Madoff had been instrumental in developing the NASDAQ stock market and served as chairman of the board of directors in 1990, 1991, and 1993. He and his brother, Peter, "have both been deeply involved in leading the dramatic transformation that has been underway [sic] in U.S. securities trading," the company boasted.

"Theses [sic] positions of leadership not only indicate the deep interest Madoff Securities has shown in its industry, they also reflect the respect the firm and its management have achieved in the financial community."

The Lipstick Building made the message clear: Bernie Madoff was a major player.

Although the building was only twelve blocks from his penthouse apartment, Madoff still kept a Fleet of black Cadillacs so he could arrive each morning in style, just like the big boys at Goldman Sachs and Morgan Stanley.

He became an investor in a restaurant just up the street, P. J. Clarke's, and always requested the table up front by the window, where everyone could see him.

In time, the firm grew to take up three floors of the Lipstick Building. The main entrance and a conference room were on the eighteenth floor. Offices for Madoff, his brother, Peter, and his sons were located on the nineteenth floor. That floor was also the location of the legitimate part of Madoff's business, where traders actually conducted a huge volume of trades in stocks for institutional customers, all overseen by Madoff's sons, Mark and Andy, and his brother, Peter. Madoff estimated that the firm handled more than a trillion dollars a year in trades.

Madoff claimed it was "the world's largest market-maker in off-exchange trading of listed U.S. equities." In 1983, Madoff opened a London trading office, which gave him the appearance of an international operation, but investigators say this was actually a front to give the impression that the seventeenth-floor schemers were buying and selling on the European market.

The legal trading part of the Madoff business bought and sold stock in the Standard & Poor's 500 Stock Index without going through the New York Stock Exchange or any other exchange. By operating independently of the formal exchanges, Madoff's firm could shave pennies or fractions of pennies off the price of a stock for its customers.

Madoff said that these institutional customers included "scores of leading securities firms and banks from across the United States and around the world." Bear Stearns was one of the firm's major clients.

Madoff was proud of his trading operation, and in 1992 he invited ABC News cameras into the office to show off his sleek, high-tech operation. Some feared that this division of his company could one day put the big stock exchanges out of business.

"The difference is that ninety-five percent of our transactions are running through our technology and are so-called untouched by human hands until such time as the execution takes place," Madoff said in a rare on-camera interview.

Steve Aug, the ABC News correspondent who interviewed Madoff, said in his report that with one hundred employees and a roomful of computers, "Madoff is now the Big Board's largest competitor, trading five percent of the stock exchange's entire share of volume."

While Madoff's name was not well known outside Wall Street, insiders knew it well.

At an industry conference in 2007, the moderator said of Madoff, "That name may not say a lot to you, but go over to Madoff and you talk to Bernie and he mentions 'Oh, by the way, ten percent of stocks traded in the United States are going through this firm right now.' It's one of those really important parts of our financial system that doesn't show up in the headlines. Most people outside of markets don't understand the role it plays, but it's a major factor in American and global financial markets today."

For Madoff, it was crucial to his image to keep up appearances, and the eighteenth and nineteenth floors reflected his obsessive-compulsive personality. He imposed a sleek black and gray color scheme on the office décor. Employees were allowed to have only one or two personal photographs on their desks, and they had to be in a Madoff-approved silver or black picture frame. All papers had to be removed from the top of the desk at the end of the day.

"His rules were he didn't want any loud colors. And he didn't want you spilling things, so he didn't want you walking around with anything that didn't have a cover on it," remembered Eleanor Squillari.

His obsession extended to the London office. Madoff had technicians install television cameras in the ceilings after he became suspicious that the employees there were taking long, liquid lunches and doing little work in the afternoons.

The veteran FBI agents who were investigating Madoff were reminded of the fastidiousness of legendary director J. Edgar Hoover, who similarly mistrusted his employees and imposed his compulsion for "tidiness" on the Bureau's offices.

When prospective clients or government regulators came to see Madoff, they would be shown into the nineteenth-floor conference room that was between Bernie's and Peter's offices. Madoff would position them so that through the room's glass wall they would see the state-of-the-art trading operation and the hustle and bustle of traders buying and selling. Few ever realized that all the activity they were witnessing was completely unconnected to Madoff's investment advisory business for wealthy clients, which was located on the seventeenth floor.

"It was very impressive and high-tech looking," recalled investment adviser Jim Hedges, who went to meet Madoff as part of a "due diligence review" for the client of a private bank considering an investment of hundreds of millions of dollars.

"I was told that this was a great opportunity to meet the Wizard of Oz behind the green curtain. And I asked him, 'There's seventy-five people behind us. Can I meet some of these guys and understand what they're doing?' recalled Hedges. "And he said no, I couldn't meet them."

According to Madoff, his legitimate trading business had $550 million in capital as of 2007, but former employees say given the small margins of profit on transactions, the business did not actually make that much money. It was, however, an excellent front or cover story for what was happening on the seventeenth floor, where lots of money was being made.

The seventeenth floor was the inner sanctum of Madoff's scam, the headquarters of the illegal operation, surrounded by great secrecy. No visitors, period. No one from the outside was going to be allowed to see behind this curtain.

Even access for Madoff employees was limited to those with a special key card. "No one really was allowed to go down there," said Eleanor.

"They had to buzz you in, if you needed to drop something off," remembered Little Rick.

Unlike his obsession with the appearance of the eighteenth and nineteenth floors, Madoff did not seem to care how the seventeenth floor looked, as long as it churned out the phony trades and statements.

None of the Madoff-mandated color schemes or desk codes applied on the seventeenth floor. People dressed like slobs. The desks and floor were always littered with stacks of papers and computer printouts.

"It looked like your crazy aunt's basement," recalled former computer tech manager Bob McMahon.

"It was just a junk shop, very dark, and it looked almost like a cave going in there because there were reams and reams of paper and stuff piled up and old computers and old screens," said McMahon.

Most of the people hired to work on the seventeenth floor had a connection to someone already employed by Madoff. It was a corporate organizational chart that read more like a family tree of wives, cousins, brothers-in-law, fiancés, lesbian lovers, neighbors, and ex-girlfriends. There were virtually no outside professionals.

"Everybody brought somebody in," recalled Little Rick, who started as a messenger in 1975 after being brought in to the Madoff office by a friend from Brooklyn. "If he trusted you, then he could trust who you brought."

Madoff had assembled a team he could trust and control. "Antisocial personalities cannot function unless they can control the people around them," said former FBI agent Brad Garrett. "You bring in some smart guy, some CPA, he's going to say 'this isn't right,' you're going to get caught." No doubt the level of knowledge and culpability varied widely, but the seventeenth floor was the "back office" where checks from clients were processed, nonexistent trades were recorded, and the bogus monthly and quarterly account statements were prepared, printed, and mailed.

While Madoff initially told the FBI he acted alone, someone had to generate the reams of paperwork necessary to fool clients and regulators into thinking everything was legitimate. These were the mechanics that made the scam possible. Investigators originally targeted between twenty-five and thirty employees, outside accountants, fund managers, and Madoff family members for possible criminal charges for their roles, even if they did not fully understand that the entire enterprise was a scam. "It would be like the prosecution of a Mafia family using the same statute," said one lawyer involved in the case. Ultimately, in addition to Bernie and Peter Madoff, thirteen other employees and associates were charged by federal prosecutors. All of them were convicted. "It would be like the prosecution of a Mafia family using the same statute," said one lawyer involved in the case. Ultimately, in addition to Bernie and Peter Madoff, thirteen other employees and associates were charged by federal prosecutors. All of them were convicted.

Two longtime Madoff employees ran the seventeenth floor: Annette Bongiorno and Frank DiPascali. They both became multimillionaires in jobs that ordinarily pay no more than a few hundred thousand dollars a year.

Annette started at Bernard L. Madoff Investment Securities as a nineteen-year-old high school graduate in the late 1960s. She was employed as Bernie's private secretary or "administrative assistant," as she liked to be known.

Annette had a team of five or six women who were responsible for preparing the monthly statements sent to clients. Many of Madoff's longtime clients would call Annette directly with questions about their accounts, and she later would earn commissions for steering new clients to Madoff through a company called RuAnn, short for her name and that of her husband, Rudy.

Former employees say Annette would often personally hand out the monthly statements to all those in the firm who had accounts with Madoff.

"She was always a welcome sight because she would be bringing the good news of another great month," said one former Madoff trader. This trader, like so many of his colleagues, lost everything when the scheme collapsed.

Referred to as the "toad" by other people in the office because she was short and overweight, Annette was once an attractive blonde whose familiar relationship with

Madoff fueled rumors about what happened between them after office hours.

"She was a cute little thing, blond hair," recalled Little Rick, who said he briefly went out with her.

Madoff allowed Annette to work from her home in Florida for months at a time, and former employees said she certainly acted as if she was protected by the boss. She acted like "the queen or the she-devil," said Little Rick, who now says she used him as a "boy toy."

"As they made more money, they got more and more to become, you know, assholes," he said of Annette and others on the seventeenth floor. "Come on, for God sakes, you know, I saw you naked. Give me a break."

She became a multimillionaire, with a $2 million home on Long Island and another million-dollar house in a gated community in Boca Raton, Florida. FBI agents told employees she had more than $70 million in investments. Among her cars are two Mercedes-Benzes and a Bentley, which sells new for $175,000. Her husband, Rudy, was an electrician for New York City's Department of Transportation for more than twenty years. In 1996 he retired on medical disability and told friends he was trading in stocks.

When an ABC News reporter approached Rudy Bongiorno outside his house following Madoff's arrest, he angrily shouted, "Don't come on my property."

Investigators came to believe that Annette was involved in the illegal scheme from the beginning of her employment, between 1967 and 1968. In her effort to cut a deal with the government, she reportedly said that "the same things she was doing in 2008 she was doing in her first year with Madoff." Only Ruth and his brother, Peter, were with Madoff longer than Annette.

Annette recruited Frank DiPascali, her next-door neighbor in the Italian working-class neighborhood of Howard Beach in Queens. According to investigators, DiPascali ultimately became even more important than Annette in the day-to-day running of the Madoff scheme. Former employees said DiPascali's ascendancy led to friction with Annette, who resented losing some of her power to Frank.

"He was a pimple-faced kid, you know?" said Little Rick, who was there when DiPascali first started working at the company in 1975 as an assistant to the managing director. "He was self-made there. He was molded there, in other words."

DiPascali worked his way up through Research and Option Trading. Titles did not mean much at the Madoff firm because they were given out on a random basis or often self-selected, but according to a résumé DiPascali submitted in 2002 to a New Jersey school system whose board he sought to join, he was promoted to chief financial officer in 1996. Investigators say that DiPascali's salary in the final years ranged between $2.25 and $3 million.

Former employees said that when Bernie came to the seventeenth floor, he would meet with Frank in one of the rooms that had the DO NOT ENTER and DO NOT CLEAN signs on the door.

Investigators say DiPascali, with a team of five others, including his brother-in-law, Robert Cardile, was in charge of producing statements reflecting thousands of trades that were supposedly being executed for Madoff's investment clients. In reality, there were no trades.

When questions were raised by suspicious investors or government investigators, it was DiPascali who would be by Madoff's side to offer elaborate fictions about the sophisticated "split strike conversion" trading strategy and computer systems supposedly being used on the seventeenth floor. He would not, however, offer any tours of his seventeenth-floor operation.

Customers were told that Madoff "would carefully time purchases and sales to maximize value" in a "basket of fifty stocks" chosen from the Standard & Poor's 100 Index, a collection of the one hundred largest publicly traded companies. The story went that sometimes Madoff would get "out of the market" and put everything in cash, in U.S. securities. To guard against a downturn, Madoff would supposedly hedge his bets by buying and selling "option contracts" matching the stocks in the basket. Under this fictional strategy, if the stocks went down, the value of the options would go up. In September 2008, DiPascali reassured one major hedge fund investor by telling him that Madoff used "twenty derivatives dealers and international banks" in their option trades. It was yet another lie.

To hear Madoff and DiPascali tell it, they had found a foolproof strategy, all carried out in great secrecy on the seventeenth floor. Investors on average received between 12- and 20-percent returns, although certain Madoff clients were rewarded with much higher rates of return. One prominent investor earned as much as 950 percent one year. Madoff said he made his profit by charging $.04 per share commission on the stocks he traded and $1.00 for every option contract he purchased.

Madoff was known to become irritated if someone asked too many questions, and he refused to answer standard industry inquiries about percentages held in cash, the amount of borrowed money, or the names of the "option counter parties."

Of course, the reason for this was that he had no good answers. The entire operation was a fabrication. No stocks were traded. No options were purchased. His profits were not coming from any $.04 stock or $1.00 option commissions.

According to the investigators, what really happened on the seventeenth floor was relatively simple. Every day, DiPascali kept track of the closing prices of the Standard & Poor's 100. Then, on a regular basis, DiPascali and Madoff would pick the stocks that had done well and create bogus trading records for their "basket of stocks."

They often got sloppy. Sometimes they recorded trades as if they had been made on weekend days or federal holidays, when the stock market was closed. None of the supposedly sophisticated investors or SEC regulators ever noticed.

Investigators would later find a consistent pattern in which Madoff and DiPascali made their fictional trades at the precise high or low price of a stock each month, an amazing feat that generated "too good to be true" profits.

Of course, it's easy to master the timing and make a profit if you already know the winners—it's like knowing which horse won the race and then placing a bet.

To help hide the fact that no trades were taking place in New York, Madoff claimed all of the trading for the investment advisory business was being done through the London office, on the European markets. Madoff regularly transferred hundreds of millions of dollars to the London office, but investigators say the London office simply wired the hundreds of millions of dollars right back to New York without buying a single share for investors. Employees in the London office later told investigators they thought their job was to buy and sell stock for Bernie's personal account. They had no idea they were supposed to be making billions in trades for the firm's investors.

Investigators say that, using a computer program, DiPascali and those who worked for him on the seventeenth floor would plug the fictional trades into the 4,900 accounts under their control. Sometimes clients needed losses for tax reasons, and Madoff and DiPascali could provide those just as easily.

Like his former neighbor Annette, DiPascali had very flexible work hours. He would show up at the office in the late morning, hardly dressed like the chief financial officer of an investment firm managing $65 billion.

"He looked to me like an electrician. He had gold chains on and he's got his pack of Marlboros in his hand and he is whizzing through the office saying hi to this person or that person," recalled the former computer tech, Bob McMahon.

"I turned to a young lady I worked with and said, 'Who is that?' and she said, 'Oh, that's Frank. He works down on seventeen. He's one of the muckety-mucks.'"

Whenever SEC auditors or big investors were around, DiPascali would show up in a suit. People on the seventeenth floor knew "something was up" in the final few weeks before Madoff's arrest because "Frankie was wearing a suit every single day."

DiPascali had long since moved from his home in Queens to a $1.3 million estate in New Jersey. He drove a Mercedes and had a large fishing boat, the *Dorothy-Jo*, with its own captain at a marina in New Jersey. According to investigators, DiPascali's boat captain, Christopher Warrin, was on the Bernard L. Madoff Investment Securities payroll, at a salary greater than many of the staff who worked in the legal area of the company.

After a long negotiation, DiPascali pleaded guilty to nine felony counts in August, 2009 and agreed to "name names and tell all" to federal prosecutors in exchange for a lighter sentence.

Former employees said DiPascali's right hand and confidante on the seventeenth floor was his deputy, JoAnn Crupi, a former waitress whom everyone called Jodi. She was a twenty-five-year veteran of the firm and arranged for her cousin, Erin Reardon, to be hired as Frank's assistant.

If Madoff needed money, he would ask his secretary to "tell Jodi to take it out of my special account." Investigators say that in 2007, Madoff took cash draws of $5 million, including one withdrawal of $2 million on a single day.

Unlike Frank and Annette, Jodi continued to come into the office after Madoff's arrest, for what some thought was "damage control." According to Madoff's secretary, Eleanor, Jodi urged employees on the seventeenth floor to stop cooperating with the FBI agents who were on the premises.

"She said she and Frank would help everyone get lawyers and the cost would be taken care of," Eleanor reported.

Like Annette and Frank, Jodi had good reason to be grateful to Bernie Madoff. Investigators say that in 2006, Madoff used $2,225,000 of investors' money to help Crupi and her partner, Judy Bowen, buy a New Jersey beach house. The money was sent to the law firm representing the women, not Crupi, and only Bowen's name appeared on the deed to the property.

Former employees said Madoff also provided Crupi with financial support when she and Bowen adopted two children from Guatemala.

In addition to generous salaries, members of the Madoff "inner circle" also were provided with Corporate Platinum American Express cards for their personal use, hardly standard practice at any legitimate corporation. Annette, Frank, and Jodi all received the cards, along with a few people from the trading floor and key Madoff family members. All the Amex charges were paid out of the bank account holding investors' money.

For example, the charge records show that DiPascali used his platinum card to buy plane tickets to the Bahamas in March 2008 for his son, Frank Jr., and four others who appeared to be his college fraternity brothers at Villanova University. They may have thanked Mr. DiPascali senior for a great spring break trip, but investigators say the money really came from Madoff's cheated investors.

"If you surround yourself with people who are beholden to you," said former FBI agent Garrett, "and you've elevated them to a position they would have probably never reached on their own, then you control them."

The corporate cards and the exorbitant salaries were kept secret from the rest of the Madoff employees. But there were always suspicions.

Computer technicians at Madoff's office thought there was something strange on the seventeenth floor because of the continued use of an old IBM AS/400 computer server, long after it was obsolete.

Nader Ibrahim used to work as a Madoff computer technician and spent a lot of time on the seventeenth floor. He remembers wondering about the outdated computer. "It's an older system, it wouldn't make sense to use such a system," he said.

It made sense only if the computer had been programmed to aid in the fraud and keeping it meant there was no need to bring in someone new to program a new computer.

"The reason why Bernie couldn't give up the AS/400 is because it was his printing press, the linchpin in the whole mix," explained Bob McMahon. "That system gets updated pricing and trading data at the end of the day. The file is created and feeds information directly for overnight processing. I was told the AS/400 was the 'books and records' of the company."

It was a tightly controlled operation, designed to be impenetrable from the outside.

On orders from Madoff, most of the computer terminals used on the seventeenth floor were not set up for e-mail. "After an SEC audit in 2006, he didn't want anyone sending any e-mails," recalled Eleanor Squillari. "A lot of people in the office had their e-mails taken away." It was all very hush-hush.

Ironically, Madoff was well known on Wall Street for

pioneering the use of computers to carry out huge trades at lightning speed. In truth, he hardly knew how to use a computer, and most of the credit for its role in the operation actually belonged to his brother, Peter. Even so, the Madoffs' advances revolutionized stock trading and led Bernie to become the chairman of NASDAQ.

Yet, on the seventeenth floor, he relied on an outdated computer and did not provide his customers with electronic real-time access to their accounts. Almost all Wall Street firms use electronic confirmations for stock trades, but Madoff used paper confirmations because they could be created after the fact—the key to his Ponzi scheme.

The use of outdated technology coupled with a beholden staff and a corporate culture of extreme secrecy enabled a business that had started with a folding card table in Queens to grow into a multibillion-dollar operation that had investors pleading to be allowed to participate. Of course, a Ponzi scheme cannot survive unless it continues to grow. The new money is needed to pay the yearly 12- to 20-percent returns to old customers.

With such great returns, year after year, a number of prominent hedge funds considered putting money with Madoff but then changed their minds after a closer look and a serious numbers crunch. According to investigators, Société Générale, Goldman Sachs, Citigroup, Morgan Stanley, Merrill Lynch, and Credit Suisse all "flatly refused to deal" with Madoff.

"There wasn't enough volume on the entire floor of

the stock exchange to support" all the trades he was supposedly making, said Suzanne Murphy, a hedge fund
investment adviser. "It told us that what he said he was
doing was not what he was actually doing."

For example, if Madoff was to be believed, on one day in
1998 he had carried out half of all the trades for the Coca-
Cola Company, a volume of trades that was not credible.

In the late 1990s, the head of the trading desk of one
major investment bank put Madoff in the fraud pool, said
Murphy, referring to a gallows humor pool that traders
use for bets on which firms are the next to be indicted.

Yet other investors continued to line up, including
some hedge fund operators who put their clients' money in
Madoff's hands in addition to their own personal fortunes.

In a way, the savviest of them may have been like
the "mark" in the film *The Sting*, the shrewd gambler
Lonnegan (Robert Shaw). He knew the character played
by Robert Redford was doing something illegal by knowing which horse had won a race before placing a bet. But it
seemed a foolproof system to score big. His greed blinded
him to the fact that he was the true target of the con.

Similarly, many of Madoff's savvy investors suspected
Madoff had his own foolproof system, which might be
illegal, but could keep those big returns coming. "A lot of
people on the street thought Madoff was front-running,"
said Murphy, referring to an illegal practice in which
traders and broker-dealers buy or sell their stocks ahead
of large orders, which are sure to drive the price. "They

could live with that—it's illegal, but if he gets caught, hey, that's not my problem."

No one wanted to find out, or challenge Bernie, Murphy says. "Don't ask Bernie too many questions because you know he doesn't like that, he gets upset."

"Every time I asked him a question, a roadblock was put up," recalled Jim Hedges. He had a two-hour meeting with Madoff in 1997. As impressive as the trading floor appeared, Hedges smelled a rat by the way Madoff reacted to his questions. "I think he was probably offended by my questions. I knew, from his level of agitation and feeling of being put-upon, that this was a very unusual dynamic. And in twenty, thirty minutes I found enough to make me say I wouldn't want my investors near this."

Like any other financial firm, Madoff also had an accounting firm, Friehling & Horowitz, whose name appeared on certified documents filed with the SEC every year, as required by law.

But Friehling & Horowitz turned out to be a three-person firm located in a strip mall in New York state's rural Rockland County, thirty miles northwest of New York City.

Of the three, only one, David Friehling, was full-time. The other employees included Friehling's part-time assistant and his father-in-law, Jerome Horowitz, living in semi-retirement in Florida. Friehling claimed to have "hundreds of clients" and to be "well respected in the community." Yet there is no evidence he had any client other than Madoff. The accounting firm's total revenue in 2008 was $180,000—a surprisingly small amount for a firm supposedly doing the accounting work for a $64.8 billion investment business.

The father-in-law, Horowitz, had been Madoff's accountant—going back to the 1960s, when Horowitz worked out of the small accounting firm on East Fortieth Street that was run by Madoff's father-in-law, Saul Alpern. Like a Mafia don, family connections were very important to Madoff.

The job of the accountant is crucial in assuring the public of the honesty and integrity of securities firms handling their money. Accountants are supposed to certify that the firm has the money it says it has, that it has made the trades it says it has, and that it has and holds the stock and securities it claims to have bought for its clients.

According to investigators, David Friehling did none of that. Instead, they say, he simply signed blank SEC forms for Madoff and others to fill in and file.

Eleanor remembers occasional visits to the office by Friehling, who also handled Madoff's personal income tax returns. "He was a nice guy, but he didn't seem to be very close to Bernie," she said.

After questions began to be raised by some investors about Friehling & Horowitz, Eleanor remembers Madoff calling Friehling to say, "You have to get an office. You cannot continue to operate out of your house." That's when he moved to his eighteen-by-thirteen office in the strip mall.

On the day after Christmas, fifteen days after Madoff's arrest, Friehling was seen removing boxes of documents from the tiny office. He was arrested by the FBI a few months later and charged with six criminal counts, including securities fraud and filing false documents with the SEC. Friehling pleaded guilty to nine criminal counts, including securities fraud, and received a relatively light sentence of time served and home detention.

Friehling's best defense about his knowledge of the scheme, or lack of knowledge, may be that he and his family members had more than $14 million in accounts with Madoff, according to the SEC. Madoff paid certain key people through the accounts, but would someone who knew it was a scam leave his family's money in those accounts? In the eight years before Madoff's arrest, more than $5 million had been withdrawn from the largest of the Friehling accounts, but much was still left—at least on paper—when Madoff was arrested. He was a victim of the very scam prosecutors say he helped cover up.

Friehling's eighty-year-old father-in-law, Jerome Horowitz, Madoff's original accountant, died of complications from cancer on the day Madoff entered his guilty plea in March, 2009.

FIVE

The Lifestyle

RUTH MADOFF WAS FURIOUS.

She had accepted the shame attached to her husband's $65 billion crime. She knew he had cheated thousands of people, including many of her close friends and family. She could handle being cut off from her social circles and even banned from her New York hair salon. She understood that the Palm Beach mansion, the oceanfront house in Montauk, and the villa and yacht on the French Riviera were gone. She was a virtual prisoner in her Manhattan penthouse. She was always afraid of running into one of her husband's former clients. She would wait for the doorman to tell her that the photographers had gone, so she could sneak out for an afternoon movie.

But Ruth could live with all that. What made her so angry one morning in late March, 2009 was an item in the *New York Daily News* claiming that ten years earlier Bernie had had an affair with a younger woman, someone in the media. Men are creeps, she fumed to people close to her after reading the article "Was Ponzi Bernie Madoff man a philanderer, too?" read the headline on the *Daily News'* Rush & Molloy gossip column. The writers said two sources confirmed Madoff's affair with "an executive assistant at a media company" who was "attractive and Jewish," according to the account. The column said Bernie was generous with her and "used to fly her around" until Ruth found out and "kept him on a short leash after that." Despite what the columnists' sources had told them, Ruth had not known about the alleged affair until the column appeared.

The story of the alleged affair spread rapidly, and the next night it provided fodder for David Letterman, who presented the Top Ten Signs Your Wife Is Having an Affair with Bernie Madoff on his late night CBS program.

Number one: "When someone on the news mentions getting screwed by Madoff, your wife says, 'Tell me about it.'"

Sitting in the luxury Manhattan penthouse made possible by her husband's crimes, Ruth seethed for days. Bernie had pleaded guilty just two weeks earlier. The judge promptly revoked his bail, ending his house arrest and sending him to jail to await his sentencing.

Ruth had vowed her love to her husband of forty-nine years and had been warming to the role of the lonely, devoted wife until she picked up that *Daily News*. Now she was experiencing the overpowering sense of betrayal and anger that Madoff's victims felt three months earlier when they learned he had cheated on them with their life savings.

At the time—three months after Bernie's arrest—Ruth had not expressed any public regrets about her husband's monumental crime or any sympathy for his victims. To the outside world, she seemed immune to the suffering of the families—including her own sister Joan's, whose finances had been devastated—or the charities that were bankrupted by Madoff's financial chicanery.

But the idea that Bernie would betray her? Cheat on her? After all she had done for him? After all they had been through together?

According to people familiar with her reaction, she vowed to get the truth from Bernie once she was allowed prison visits. And, in fact, a few weeks later, when she visited him at the federal Metropolitan Correctional Center in Lower Manhattan, he denied the affair. And she believed him. She was sorry she had even brought it up. Her Bernie would not lie to her. After all, he wasn't a creep. He was still that tan, handsome lifeguard who had swept her off her feet at a beach in Queens fifty years earlier.

Life in the ensuing decades had been very good for

Ruth and Bernie. Once Bernie's scheme was in place, there had never been any shortage of money. In some cases, tens of millions of dollars would suddenly appear in Ruth's accounts with no apparent explanation, according to investigators.

In addition to swindling his investors, investigators say there is evidence he stole from some of them outright by looting the estates of clients who had named him the executor.

On their most recent federal income tax return, for 2007, the Madoffs reported $13,262,706 in gross income. His salary from the company was $9,422,238. They collected tax-free interest of $2,566,428 from some $45 million in municipal bonds. He knew better than to put that money in the hands of the seventeenth floor.

Their IRS 1040 return was prepared by David Friehling, the same small-town accountant who is suspected of covering up Madoff's fraud at Bernard L. Madoff Investment Securities. It is full of typographical errors.

Madoff may have cut corners in hiring an accountant, but he spared no expense in catering to his and Ruth's every whim or desire.

They traveled the world together in two private luxury jets co-owned by Madoff with family and friends. Bernie and Ruth adopted a style and demeanor that belied their outer-borough upbringing. They sought the "old money" look, even though their money was freshly stolen.

His clothes were expensive and elegant. Dark blues and grays with a black knit tie. He looked like a French diplomat. On a shopping spree weeks before his downfall, Madoff spent several thousand dollars at Trillion, a men's store in Palm Beach, where he chose a $1,200 blue Polo shirt and a $2,000 pair of light gray cashmere slacks.

"That's Bernie's shade," said co-owner David Neff.

For shoes, Madoff was a loyal customer of Belgian Shoes, located just down the street from his office. Since 1979, Madoff had bought dozens of handmade suede loafers for around $350 a pair. He told people it was the only shoe he would wear.

Madoff was obsessive about his appearance. Often, when he bought a pair of the shoes, or any tie or shirt, he would buy ten of each item. There would be one each for the meticulous walk-in closets at his four homes in Manhattan, Montauk, Palm Beach, and the French Riviera. The other six sets of clothes were for the six steamer trunks he bought and shipped to his six favorite hotels around the world, including The Lanesborough in London, the Plaza Athénée in Paris, and the Hôtel du Cap-Eden-Roc on the Riviera, so that when Madoff traveled to his favorite places, he took no clothes; they were waiting for him.

"Someone who plans ahead so well that he pre-positions his clothes around the world, don't you think he has some hidden bank accounts around the world, too?" asked one investigator on the case.

In the last ten years, Bernie and Ruth's life had been a wonderful merry-go-round, with stops in the Hamptons; Palm Beach; the Riviera; Cabo San Lucas, Mexico; and skiing in St. Moritz, Vail, and Aspen. Bernie was the "non-skiing" captain of the ski team for the Cincinnati stock exchange, which he and his brother helped transform into the National Stock Exchange.

"We had these meetings around the world where all of the stock exchanges of the world would get together for one week and end up with a big gala and ski competition," said Nando Pignatelli, a former broker from Monte Carlo. Bernie "was seen with very good-looking girls, but they and their husbands were part of the team. He had Ruth there as his wife. Peter with his wife. They were absolutely very regular."

When they weren't vacationing in exclusive locations around the world, they maintained their luxury lifestyle at home in New York City. Their penthouse apartment at 133 E. 64th Street, on Manhattan's Upper East Side, was an understated showcase. Valued at $7.5 million, it is a two-story expanse on the eleventh and twelfth floors. They moved into the city from their suburban home in Roslyn, Long Island, after their sons, Mark and Andy, had finished school. In a building full of millionaires, Madoff was on the top floor, with a commanding view of the city. One of the couple's close friends, Susan Blumenfeld, served as the decorator. On her Web site, Blumenfeld boasts of her "artistic prowess" and ability to "customize any space to reflect each client's character with an unexpected flair that is always elegant and beautiful." She also was the decorator for Madoff's offices and his yacht.

For the New York apartment, Blumenfeld chose a neutral color palette, with antique Oriental rugs and classic furnishings. As in the office, there were no loud colors—nothing flashy for the Madoffs.

There was a Steinway grand piano in the living room on the top floor, along with floor-to-ceiling windows and a fireplace. Small statues of bulls were placed on each side of the entrance to the room. Nearby was a formal dining room with its own fireplace, a crystal chandelier, and a $64,000 set of silverware. The large eat-in kitchen adjoined the room where Madoff spent most of his time after the arrest, reading the paper and watching old movies on a large flat-screen television. Visitors said the apartment was spotless. According to investigators, the Madoffs' housekeeper, Praxides Dirilo, was paid out of the company accounts.

The bedrooms were on the eleventh floor, accessed by a large spiral staircase. Bernie and Ruth each had a personal walk-in dressing closet for their expensive wardrobes. Bernie arranged his suits, hand-tailored in London, precisely one inch apart. Each shirt had its own pull-out shelf, and his twenty pairs of suede loafers were arrayed as if on retail display. Down the hall, the master bathroom was big enough for an exercise bike and a large flatscreen television. Bernie and Ruth also had their own luxurious dens. His was all mahogany and decorated with a nautical theme and a leather sofa. There was a metal statue of a bull on the floor. Her den featured an equestrian motif, with Chinese lacquer and floral fabric for the sofa. While he was under house arrest, ABC News cameras from across the street saw both Madoffs relaxing in her den, watching television, surfing the Internet on an Apple computer, and then fluffing the thick pillows on the sofa before turning out the lights and going to bed.

The oceanfront home in Montauk, on New York's Long Island, was their summer getaway place, purchased in the early 1980s. It is a sprawling estate with its own beach, on Old Montauk Highway. The Madoffs held a yearly summer party for the office in Montauk, but after one particularly raucous weekend, the event was shifted from the family home to nearby motels.

The office summer party began as a fishing trip in the 1980s, and it grew into a three-day beach extravaganza. Employees and their families were all put up at area beach motels. At the last party, in mid-July 2008, there was a beach bonfire dinner on Friday night. Saturday was spent on the sand, with clowns, games, and face painting for the children. Bernie and Ruth sat in beach chairs under a set of umbrellas, as if they were the king and the queen watching their loyal subjects from their thrones. On Saturday night, the festivities moved to the nearby

Montauk Yacht Club for an elegant dinner under a huge tent, with a DJ playing music for dancing.

It was the social highlight of the year for the office, and it allowed Madoff to be seen as the great benefactor. Former employees remembered that Madoff loved to watch everyone dance as they stopped, started, and jumped up and down on the commands of someone with a loud whistle.

His messenger, Little Rick, remembers Bernie smoking joints during some of the beach parties, seemingly able to relax and forget for a moment the huge scam he was juggling. Many of those same people he so enjoyed watching on the dance floor, or playing with their children at the beach, invested their savings with Madoff. When they lost everything, they wondered how he could have done it to them when he had always appeared to be such a kind and thoughtful man.

"You would have liked him," said one former Madoff trader whose savings were wiped out in the scam.

"We thought we were working for this wonderful man. We thought we were doing the right thing for our families. And we just thought that we were having a nice life. And we weren't," said Eleanor Squillari. "I never could picture him as wanting to hurt innocent people, but clearly he did, and clearly he knew he was doing it," she said with anger as she recalled all the good times at the Montauk summer parties.

In the winter, the Madoffs spent their weekends,

holidays, and long stretches in Palm Beach. It's an easy commute from New York when a private jet is standing by. The Madoffs first bought a condominium in the area that some longtime residents in Palm Beach called the "Gaza Strip" because of the perception that most of the newcomers in the high-rise condos were Jewish, intruding on this WASP stronghold.

In 1994, as business was booming and the threat of an SEC investigation had passed, Madoff paid $8 million for a waterfront home on the very fashionable Lake Way. He was one of the first Jewish homeowners in that part of town.

The house at 410 N. Lake Way seems to attract the notorious. It was previously owned by Herbert "Peter" and Roxanne Pulitzer, whose sensational divorce trial included testimony about sexual escapades in the house involving three-way partnerships and a long list of other titillating details. One witness testified that Roxanne Pulitzer had séances on her bed with a trumpet nearby, and she was soon described by the New York tabloids as "the Strumpet with the Trumpet." Bernie and Ruth couldn't top that for sensationalism, but their infamy may prove to be more enduring.

The Madoffs joined the Palm Beach Country Club, whose membership was mostly Jewish. All members were major contributors to charities—it was one of the requirements for membership. On their 2007 federal tax return, the Madoffs reported more than $8 million in charitable contributions to a variety of organizations, although much of it was given to foundations established in the name of Bernard L. Madoff and his son Mark Madoff. In 2007, The Madoff Family Foundation had more than $19 million in assets and distributed only $95,000, less than 1 percent.

The Madoffs met their country club's definition of being charitable, although in their case they were giving away other people's money. Ruth Madoff often used the Corporate Platinum American Express card to make charitable contributions in smaller amounts.

Members of the Palm Beach Country Club remember Madoff acting like royalty at the clubhouse. To know him, and be accepted by him as an investor, was to be in the elite of the elite. Multimillionaires in the club said they were hesitant to approach him directly for fear of causing offense. Someone had to recommend you.

"It's almost like you've got to grovel. 'Come to me, I'm the king,'" said former FBI agent Brad Garrett. "That's extremely important to people with antisocial personality problems. 'You're going to have to do what I say and maybe I'll help you and maybe I won't.'"

The Madoffs were members of several other golf country clubs, including the Atlantic Golf Club in Bridgehampton, New York. Investigators discovered that Bernie used clients' money to pay $947,703 in country club dues for himself, his brother, Peter, and their wives between 1996 and 2008.

Bernie was considered an above-average golfer, with a nine handicap, according to people who played with him regularly. Ruth was also above average and often played with Bernie, defying the belief of many golfers that love and golf don't mix.

They enjoyed each other's company. Some of Ruth's most treasured memories are of weekends spent alone with Bernie in their New York apartment. This was not a couple who sought separate vacations or a little breathing room from each other.

"They were incredibly close," said Eleanor. "I think they genuinely loved and liked each other. Which is huge, when you're together for so long. They did everything together. He wanted to be with her. The movies, and dinners, even a quiet dinner at home."

Still, according to former employees, Ruth was well aware that Bernie had a wandering eye.

She surprised him once at an industry cocktail party, where Bernie was "getting a little frisky" with another woman, recalls Little Rick. "Bernie's there and Peter's there and they've both got blondes next to them, and who walks into the place—in dungarees and a T-shirt no less—but Ruth Madoff.

"She takes one look and she was out. There was no scene. She was a very sophisticated, very classy lady. Needless to say, after that day, everybody went to the industry dinner, all the wives, everybody."

Little Rick says Ruth kept a very close eye on Bernie after that. As he served as a chauffeur one day, he heard Bernie ask Ruth, "So, honey, when you coming back?"

"She goes, 'You think I'm gonna tell you when I'm coming back?'

"I wanted to turn around, tell him, 'She knows your ass real good,'" Little Rick said.

Madoff also had a loyal team of attractive female masseuses. His "little black book," a $415 goatskin version from the French leather goods store Hermès, contained nine women, under M, who provided massages, in New York, Montauk, Florida, and France.

"I did tell Bernie if he loses that book that somebody's gonna think he's a pervert," said Eleanor, who kept a separate copy of the address book and provided it to the FBI.

In the book, the Madoff number for "Lena" traces to a sexually explicit Web site, where "Lena" is also called "Lilly." On the site, customers say they paid $150 for a "nude" massage. "The massage was very good and she used her tits and hair to add to the sensual feel. I loved it," wrote one satisfied client.

Other female masseuses have Web sites that state they are "non-sexual." Bernie's former messenger, Little Rick, said Madoff told him he often liked to watch "one woman massage another."

The stories of Madoff with other escort service women, hotel masseuses, and certain attractive female employees were well known around the office. According to former employees, this was especially true in the 1980s. Ruth learned to live with it.

She could find her consolation in her status as Mrs. Madoff, the wife of one of Wall Street's most successful investment strategists. Their presence was sought after by hostesses in Manhattan, the Hamptons, and Palm Beach. Her Corporate Platinum Amex card allowed her to buy whatever she wanted, whenever she wanted. In January 2008, company documents show that Ruth spent $3,792 on a one-day Paris stroll from Giorgio Armani to Jil Sander to Marni.

And she made sure to send word back to the old neighborhood about just how wealthy she and Bernie were getting.

Bernie's childhood friend Jay Portnoy says his mother received regular updates from Ruth's mother, Sara Alpern, and Bernie's mother, Sylvia. "I was often told, 'Mrs. Alpern says Bernie's doing very well in the stock market,' 'Mrs. Madoff says Bernie's now doing extremely well,' 'Mrs. Alpern says Bernie's now a millionaire,' and then a multimillionaire."

By 2006, at the age of sixty-eight, Madoff had enough money and free time to enjoy a fourth home, this time on the French Riviera. The Chase Bank corporate account had several billion dollars in it, enough to handle the continued 12- to 20-percent returns and the occasional client withdrawal. Under Frank and Annette's supervision, the seventeenth floor was operating like a well-oiled machine. Madoff could take time away from the office without fear of the scheme collapsing. He and Ruth loved France— especially the Riviera.

Bernie and Ruth had traveled there often, staying at the Hôtel du Cap-Eden-Roc in Cap d'Antibes, between Cannes and Nice. It is one of the most elegant hotels in the world, built on a cliff overlooking the Mediterranean and surrounded by a forest of pines. The yachts line up along the waterfront so that their owners can be ferried to the hotel's outdoor terrace for lunch next to the pool. It was Bernie Madoff's kind of place.

The Madoff villa was nearby, in an area of Cap d'Antibes known as Château des Pins.

Ruth and Bernie spent a lot of time and money collecting antiques and art for their French villa: a $35,000 painting bought at The Armory Show in New York, furniture from hidden Parisian shops, a leather chair from London. The villa was modest by the standards of many of the Riviera's grand estates, but the Madoffs loved it.

"Nothing flashy at all," said Nando Pignatelli, the former stockbroker who often visited at the Madoffs' place. "Don't forget that I live in Monte Carlo, and I know what these rich people are and want to look like when they want to show off. He was never a show-off."

Madoff's most prized possession was the eighty-eight-foot yacht he bought for about $7.5 million in 2007, named *The Bull*. He docked it at Juan-les-Pins in Cap d'Antibes, near the Riviera villa. His New York decorator, Susan Blumenfeld, decorated it for the Madoffs, and Bernie commissioned an oil painting of the vessel. Now he could be delivered by sea to the Hôtel du Cap's terrace like the other wealthy residents of the area.

He now had a yacht on the Riviera, part ownership of two private jets, four multimillion-dollar homes, access to a bank account with billions of dollars in it, and no way out of the monumental crime scheme that had made it all possible.

After his arrest, Bernie was asked how he had planned to end his Ponzi scheme, what was his exit strategy?

"I just somehow hoped the world would end, that would have been a way out," he told a visitor.

"But Bernie," the visitor said, "that would mean that Ruth and the boys and the grandkids would all be dead."

"Right," said Bernie.

Ruth seemed oblivious to any problem, even though they otherwise seemed so close.

"As far as I know, there was nothing that they kept from each other since they were teenagers," said Eleanor.

Ruth had helped Bernie run the business when he started it. Her father steered him some of his first clients. Ruth's role had diminished over the years, but she still had her own office one floor below Bernie's. Former employees have told investigators that she was there at least once or twice a week.

At one point, she went back to school to study nutrition and received a master's degree from New York University. She is also listed as one of the two executive editors of a cookbook called *Great Chefs of America Cook Kosher*, though her precise role in the book's creation is in dispute. Although Ruth and her co-executive editor appear in a photograph wearing aprons in a kitchen, the editor of the book, Karen MacNeil, told ABC News that she wrote and assembled the book and its recipes herself and never once met or talked with Ruth.

Mostly, when Bernie went to the office, Ruth seemed to be a rich wife who had lunch, played golf, played bridge at the club, worked out at the Equinox gym, and enjoyed her wine and a smoke. She did not seem to have a care in the world other than making sure all the help was paid.

"People like Madoff pick people in their lives who stay with them. Who are basically codependent," said former FBI agent Garrett. The type of person who thinks, "'I don't really want to know what you're up to, but I do want to benefit with the yachts and clothes and houses and antiques.'"

In the weeks before her husband's arrest, Ruth emptied her accounts of $15.5 million and helped Bernie prepare for the collapse. If she didn't know it then, she would soon realize that she was married to a crook, and yet she remained close and loyal. Still in love, she said.

"When your life becomes this sort of mega-materialism

and there's really no reality in your life," said Garrett, "you can basically rationalize away all those things around, outside this world of wealth and materialism that you're entitled to."

When reality hit, Ruth would be devastated.

"OBVIOUSLY, FIRST OF ALL, THIS CONVERSATION NEVER took place, Mark, okay?" Bernie Madoff warned the man on the other end of the line.

"Yes, of course."

It was December 19, 2005, and for the first time in more than a decade, Madoff was facing the prospect that he might get caught by the Securities and Exchange Commission, which has broad powers to investigate the financial industry.

The SEC investigators were due to arrive in a few days, and Madoff was on the phone, coaching a witness, Mark McKeefrey, on how to outsmart their questions.

Madoff repeated his warning, "this conversation never took place."

Madoff was tense. His criminal scheme was booming. Customers were happy, and there were billions of dollars in the Chase account—more than enough to pay out the huge returns he had promised. The only thing other than a market crash that could get in his way was the SEC. And now they were at the door.

Madoff had had close calls before. His scheme had narrowly survived the economic downfall triggered by the 9/11 attacks in 2001. Because he never bought or sold any stock, he did not really care what the market did. But the tough post-9/11 market led huge numbers of his customers to withdraw their money from him, and the Chase account bank balance had become precipitously low. Investigators say Madoff hid this liquidity shortfall by repeatedly sending bank wire transfers of hundreds of millions of dollars to his London office, which then immediately wired the money back to him. It was a Madoff version of "kiting checks." The SEC did not notice, and no one at the firm or its banks raised a red flag.

Madoff's last close call had come in 1992, when the SEC investigated the accounting firms of Avellino & Bienes and Telfran Associates, who had been steering millions of dollars to Madoff. But the accountants had received only civil fines, and the SEC did not pursue Madoff's "too good to be true" returns of 12 to 20 percent a year. As a result, Madoff's name never appeared in any of the SEC's public documents back then. The perception of many investors, in fact, was that the SEC investigation cleared Madoff of any suspicion of wrongdoing. There was a flattering article in the *Wall Street Journal* and new customers pleaded for Bernie to take their money.

In 2004 the SEC initiated, but then shut down, an inquiry into allegations that Madoff was "front-running," the illegal practice in which brokers place their own orders to buy and sell before their customers. The SEC dropped the case after "higher-ups" apparently decided all investigative resources should be focused on the unrelated allegations that mutual funds were playing fast and loose with their money.

But now, in 2005, Madoff sensed he was again in the cross hairs of the SEC.

Investigators planned to interview Amit Vijayvergiya, the chief risk officer of the Fairfield Greenwich Group, headquartered in New York City, with offices in Greenwich, Connecticut. Fairfield Greenwich Group is a giant hedge fund that had steered billions of dollars from its clients to Madoff. They were Madoff's single biggest customer, with accounts totaling some $7.2 billion.

Any close examination of the books would reveal lots of loose ends and contradictions about how Fairfield Greenwich's money was invested by Madoff. If these records were pulled and pursued, Madoff knew it could be his undoing. It was essential that Madoff and Fairfield Greenwich get their stories straight.

On the call with the worried Madoff was Vijayvergiya, from the Fairfield Greenwich offices in Bermuda, and McKeefrey, the Fairfield Greenwich general counsel and chief operating officer at the New York headquarters. Lawyers for Fairfield Greenwich had already disclosed to the SEC that they were going to contact Madoff. The SEC apparently had no objection, although it seems unlikely they would have approved the conversation that followed.

Madoff took Vijayvergiya through what he should say in response to certain technical questions and advised him, most of all, to act casual with the SEC examiners.

"With these guys, anything you can't answer you basically just say I, you know, don't answer. You know, you just say, you know, I'm not knowledgeable in that aspect of it," Madoff advised as he spelled out how to deflect and bamboozle the SEC.

"But as I say, with them, you don't offer anything unless they . . . ," said Madoff, whose sentence was finished by the cooperative Vijayvergiya.

". . . unless they ask," said Vijayvergiya.

Among Madoff's most important skills was his ability to co-opt, outwit, and calmly lie to the SEC and others who might have uncovered his fraud. He worked hard at infiltrating and ingratiating himself with the very government and industry agencies that were supposed to investigate him.

Madoff had served as the chairman of the board of

directors of the NASDAQ stock exchange for three one-year terms, and as chairman or member of nine other boards at the National Association of Securities Dealers (NASD). As such, he was a man to be reckoned with—especially by the industry regulators who worked for the NASD. NASD is now called the Financial Industry Regulatory Authority (FINRA).

Either FINRA or NASD took "regulatory action" against Madoff's broker-dealer trading operation for relatively minor procedural infractions in 1963, 1975, 2005, 2007, and 2008. Even though Madoff Investment Securities was all one big firm in the same building, FINRA said it had no jurisdiction to investigate the investment advisory side of the business. And so Madoff's fraud continued unchecked.

Madoff also made sure to be an active presence at another major industry group, the Securities Industry Association, where he chaired the trading committee. His brother, Peter, also served on the board of that group, which later merged to be known as the Securities Industry and Financial Markets Association. (Peter was forced to resign his position when Bernie was arrested.)

Bernie and Peter reportedly provided tens of thousands of dollars for conferences set up by the Securities Industry Association. Who could ever suspect the man funding the industry oversight organization of wrongdoing?

At an industry conference on regulation in 2007, Madoff spoke as if there was no way for any fraud to last for long. "If you read things in the newspaper, and you see somebody violate a rule you say, Well, they're always doing this, but it's impossible for a violation to go undetected. Certainly not for a considerable period of time," said the man who, at the very same time, was decades into carrying out the largest fraud scheme in Wall Street history.

Similarly, Madoff cultivated important relationships with the SEC and its top officials.

In 2000 Madoff was asked to help an SEC advisory committee dealing with stock market rules in the wake of electronic trading.

The Madoff "little black book"—the book of essential contacts that he never traveled without—also included the misspelled name of a senior SEC official, Mike Macchiaroli, and the correct, direct line number for his Washington office. He is the associate director in the office of Broker Dealer Finances, in the Trading and Market Division.

Investigators were surprised to find Macchiaroli's name in Madoff's book, and wondered why a senior SEC official was considered one of Madoff's "essential contacts." They said that Macchiaroli had been a respected, behind-the-scenes presence at the SEC for years. "He was in market regulations, which doesn't do the investigations, but when the enforcement people received a tip or a complaint about Madoff, he would have been the kind of person they might run it by," said one of the investigators on the case.

The question was whether Macchiaroli did anything to help Madoff. Did he come to Madoff's defense? David Kotz, the SEC inspector general, received a copy of Madoff's "little black book" from the FBI and was asking the same questions. Madoff had badly misspelled Macchiaroli's name—*Macrioli*—so the relationship couldn't have been that close, and investigators found that Madoff often made more of his connections to the SEC than there was in reality. Still, given the SEC missteps in the various investigations of Madoff, the appearance of Macchiaroli's name in the book caused agents to wonder.

When asked, Macchiaroli first said he had "nothing to do with enforcement" and denied that he had any "close relationship" with Madoff and had "only met him once or twice on the street."

Madoff's secretary, Eleanor Squillari, said she doubts that. "He wouldn't be in Bernie's address book if Bernie didn't need his number. If he only spoke to the man once, or only ran into him in the street, there's no way he would be in that book. I'm not saying the man is lying, I'm just saying I know Bernie's habits."

In a later conversation, Macchiaroli said it was no surprise that he would be in Madoff's address book, and he recalled a more extensive set of contacts with Madoff—going back to at least 1987. "During the crash in '87, for example, I called all of the firms. Madoff was one of the firms we called to see how they were doing, how they were coping, and Madoff knew me." Macchiaroli said "I don't recall" if anyone from the enforcement division had ever contacted him about Madoff, but he said he had always had a high opinion of Madoff. "I know the same things that other people know. You look at him, he looks like a grandfather, treats everybody very nicely." But Macchiaroli was adamant that he was not involved in any way in helping Madoff avoid investigation by his agency.

"What the hell would I have done for him?" asked Macchiaroli.

Madoff had another, perhaps even more important, connection to the SEC, through his niece, Shana, who was the firm's compliance lawyer. Shana's love life became a focus of the investigation after her uncle's arrest. In 2007, Shana married Eric Swanson, a ten-year veteran of the SEC, who was the assistant director in the Office of Compliance Inspections and Examinations' market oversight unit in Washington. He supervised "the commission's inspection program responsible for regulatory oversight of trading on the securities exchange."

In his official capacity, Swanson would have known Shana's uncle well. His office conducted regular inspections of all broker-dealers, including Madoff, and Swanson was the SEC official who approved the 2003–2004 "front-running" investigation of Madoff that was abruptly halted. Swanson says another official had already taken over the case when it was stopped and that he played no role in that decision.

In April 2006, friends say that Eric asked Shana out for a drink and it quickly became serious. At the time, the separate SEC investigation of the Ponzi scheme allegations was going full tilt in New York and investigators had already concluded that Shana's uncle Bernie had "mislead" (sic) them.

Shana and Eric had known each other from attending various industry conferences that dealt with the rather arcane SEC compliance rules relating to the Madoff firm's legitimate trading operation. At the time of their first date, Shana had spent the last year and a half attending to her dying brother, Roger, who was suffering from leukemia. He would die two weeks later.

"Shana and Eric were really an unlikely match," said one family friend. "He was a schmuck from the Midwest, and she was this divorced New York lawyer into yoga. But her brother's death had a big impact on her, and she and Eric really found each other."

Four months after their first date, Swanson submitted his resignation to the SEC and moved to New York to live with Shana. They were married in September 2007. One Madoff family friend who attended the wedding recalled that "half of the frickin' SEC seemed to be there. On one side there was the Madoff family, and on the other the SEC."

An employee from Madoff's London office who attended the wedding said that Madoff looked at all the SEC officials in attendance and said, "That's the enemy."

Former employees said that Shana was not everyone's favorite in the office. "She appeared to be very spoiled," said Eleanor, who had known her since she was a child and was actually fond of her. Shana's uncle was the boss and her father, Peter, was second-in-command. "If you're raised in that kind of an environment, and your parents spoil you, you're gonna have a different way and a different air about you."

Her marriage to an SEC official was quite a coup for Madoff, and it came just two months before the SEC office in New York formally closed its investigation of the firm, finding no Ponzi scheme.

Madoff boasted about the relationship between Shana and Eric at a 2007 industry conference on the markets and government regulators. "So there's always this friction that goes on between the regulation side of the industry and the practitioners that say okay, where do you draw the line?" Madoff said. "I'm very close with the regulators so I'm not trying to say that what they do is bad. As a matter of fact, my niece just married one," he said to laughter.

"My condolences," said trader Muriel Siebert, whose own trading company was on the same floor of the Lipstick Building with Madoff.

"Did the SEC approve?" asked another panelist.

"He's an attorney," Madoff said as the laughter continued.

When Madoff's scheme was exposed one year later and the failure of the SEC to detect it became known, the marriage was no longer a laughing matter.

The SEC inspector general, David Kotz, launched a full investigation into the SEC's failure to detect the crime and Madoff's dealings with people at the agency, including Swanson. Kotz interviewed Madoff for three hours in New York in June 2009, and included questions about his niece's marriage, but the inspector general told prosecutors that Madoff's information was of little value and would not "shape and fortify the future of Wall Street regulation and oversight."

Friends said Swanson was devastated to be linked in any way to questions of corruption and he even hired a public relations adviser. "Swanson did not participate in New York's investigation and didn't seek to influence the outcome," said family spokesman Eric Starkman of Starkman Associates.

Even if the relationship was as innocent and unconnected to the SEC's oversight as Swanson and Madoff maintain, it served to underscore the cozy relationship that Madoff's firm enjoyed with the principal government regulator of financial institutions, the SEC.

"He charmed the pants off of everybody, including everybody at the SEC. There came a point where the SEC would call me every year to have the interns come to take a tour of our office," Eleanor said. "And we were more than happy to accommodate." Bernie or Peter or one of Bernie's sons would meet the interns and give them a full tour as a future generation of SEC auditors fell under the Madoff spell.

When SEC investigators were in the building to conduct routine audits, Madoff insisted that they not leave the conference room they had been assigned to. They were told that they could have anything they wanted, but Madoff also told Eleanor to keep an eye on them. Their comings and goings were closely noted and reported to Madoff. "If any calls came into the office for them, they would go through me and I would let Bernie know who was calling," Eleanor said. "If they were gonna make copies, I would offer to do the copies for them and let Bernie know what they were copying." Other than the men's room, they were not allowed to go anywhere else in the office. They also weren't permitted to have any "unauthorized" discussions with any employees.

Eleanor says that the SEC auditors accepted their role and did not complain.

Out of their sight, however, Bernie would be a nervous wreck, appearing to his secretary to be preoccupied, "just staring out the window; just seemed to be waiting, waiting for them to finish."

Madoff knew better than anyone what was at stake. A

simple slip or a glance at the wrong document could bring down his empire.

"He always said, 'My reputation is my business.' Of course, now I know, and I got to tell you, even for somebody who was sitting there staring out into space, he remained pretty calm. I find that pretty incredible. I don't know how the man slept at night," Eleanor said.

The investigation that began in 2005 and continued through all of 2006 and most of 2007 was a dangerous one for Madoff. At one point he thought he had been caught.

The SEC opened what it called an "initial inquiry" in late 2005. It turned into a full investigation in January 2006, based on serious allegations from an "independent fraud investigator" who claimed that Madoff's investment strategy was nothing but a Ponzi scheme, and from the SEC's own staff, which reported that "Bernard L. Madoff—mislead [sic] the examination staff" about the nature of his investment strategy.

The "independent fraud investigator" was Harry Markopolos, who first contacted the SEC Boston office about Madoff in May 2000 and continued to raise questions until he finally sent the SEC a twenty-page report entitled "The World's Largest Hedge Fund Is a Fraud" in 2005.

Markopolos became intrigued, and then puzzled, and then suspicious of Madoff's unparalleled success. He worked for a Madoff rival who wanted Markopolos to figure out Bernie's secret of success. When he and a colleague, Neil Chelo, tried to replicate trades using Madoff's stated "split strike conversion" trading strategy, they found it was impossible.

As he analyzed the public filings, Markopolos could not understand why Madoff had only had $160 million in U.S. Treasury notes when, in other documents, he claimed his portfolio had $1.147 billion in U.S. Treasury notes. "Where did the missing $1 billion go???" he wrote to Chelo. "There's more holes in the Madoff portfolio than all the golf courses in Florida."

Markopolos and Chelo ran the numbers again and again and finally concluded the former chairman of the NASDAQ stock exchange was running a Ponzi scheme.

"In less than four hours I knew I had proved mathematically that [Bernard Madoff] was a fraud," Markopolos said.

"You simply could not run that amount of money in that strategy and make those types of returns," said Chelo.

Chelo even challenged Amit Vijayvergiya, the risk manager at Fairfield Greenwich, who told him that Madoff was just exceptionally skilled. "Bernie is long when the markets go up and out of the market when it is not favorable," Chelo said he was told. "So for seventeen years, he has had perfect market timing," wrote Chelo. Nobody, ever, had been that good.

Markopolos repeatedly submitted his findings and concerns to the SEC in Boston and New York. He later testified to Congress that "the SEC never called me. I had to call the SEC repeatedly in order to try to move the case forward and with little to no response." He described the branch chief of the New York SEC office, Meaghan Cheung, as incompetent and rude. "Ms. Cheung also never grasped any of the concepts in my report, nor was she ambitious enough or courteous enough to ask questions of me. Her arrogance was highly unprofessional given my understanding of her responsibility and mandate."

At the SEC offices, Markopolos's strident tone and claims that his life was in jeopardy did not help his credibility. Some thought he was a "kook" and "obsessed with Madoff."

Markopolos picked up on the skepticism at the SEC. "Every phone call to Meaghan Cheung made me feel diminished as a person," he said.

Finally, in late 2005, after years of ignoring him, the SEC launched an initial inquiry based on Markopolos's twenty-page report sent on October 25. In the document, Markopolos concluded that Madoff was conducting one of two frauds. Either he was "front-running," using knowledge of other trades to place his trades first, or, "highly likely," wrote Markopolos, "Madoff Securities is the world's largest Ponzi Scheme." He wrote that three full years before Madoff would be arrested.

Even though the SEC could no longer ignore Markopolos's well-documented findings, it still pulled its punches and continued to be skeptical that the esteemed Bernard Madoff could be a crook. Markopolos was characterized in the case file as "neither a BLM insider nor an aggrieved investor," and members of the SEC said the commission only opened the investigation "in an abundance of caution."

Instead of issuing subpoenas for Madoff's documents and records, the staff only requested "voluntary production of certain documents," trusting Madoff to comply fully and honestly.

According to e-mails discovered later by investigators, this gave Madoff plenty of time for the seventeenth floor to create reams of phony computer runs, which had the desired effect of fooling the SEC people in the office.

The SEC staff also decided to conduct "voluntary interviews" with Madoff and his assistant, Frank DiPascali, as well as Amit Vijayvergiya at Fairfield Greenwich, who was being extensively coached by Madoff about what to say. For some reason, Fairfield Greenwich taped the phone conversation and turned over the tape when subpoenaed by the secretary of the commonwealth, who launched his own investigation because of the huge losses suffered by the people in his state. The tapes provided yet another example of Madoff trying to manipulate others to help him deceive the SEC.

"Your position," said Madoff at another point in the conversation, "is say, listen, Madoff has been in business for forty-five years; you know, he executes, you know, a huge percentage of the industry's orders, he's—you know, he's a well-known broker. You know, we make the assumption that he's—he's doing everything properly."

Madoff then instructed Vijayvergiya to keep away from answers that might reveal that Madoff was actually acting as an investment adviser. The SEC requires investment advisers to formally register, and Madoff had never done that in his five decades of serving as one. Now it was important to Madoff that he not be seen as the wizard who was making all the big decisions about what to buy and sell.

"I mean, the idea is that it's—is that we're not the one that's making the decision how much to—I mean, you know—you know, we're not the one that's operating the fund," Madoff coached Vijayvergiya.

At one point in the two-hour conversation, Madoff put the two men from Fairfield Greenwich on hold. He apologized when he came back on the line. "I'm sorry, if I get anymore solicitations for charity, I'm going to kill myself," Madoff said.

Finally, Madoff told Vijayvergiya not to worry, that the SEC "has no idea what the hell is going on" in the rapidly changing financial landscape. "The guys come in to do a books and records examination and they—they whatchamacallit—you know, they ask you a zillion different questions and we look at them sometimes and we laugh, and we say, are you guys writing a book?"

Madoff's contempt for the SEC investigators was

deep. "These guys, they work for five years at the commission, then they become a compliance manager at a hedge fund now."

"Right," said the Fairfield Greenwich risk manager. "Or they—they go work for proprietary trading desk. Nobody wants to stay there forever," Madoff said. Madoff knew the power of greed.

Remember, said Madoff, "you're best off just being, you know, casual."

"We're trying," responded the Fairfield Greenwich lawyer Mark McKeefrey. "We're trying to be cool and to just cooperate and get it over with and get them out of here."

Vijayvergiya was interviewed on December 21, 2005, and the Fairfield Greenwich executives later gave Madoff a full report on the testimony. According to the Fairfield Greenwich lawyers, Vijayvergiya "did not follow Madoff's implied suggestion, but rather told the SEC during the interview about his recent conversation with Madoff." The Massachusetts secretary of state, William Galvin, says the transcript reveals a lot more than an "implied suggestion" from Madoff.

"They followed his instructions, they followed his coaching," said Galvin. "If there's anything remarkable about that conversation beyond his brazenness, it was how confident he was that he could steer them into deceiving the SEC."

When the SEC interviewed Madoff "voluntarily" on May 19, 2006, he spun hours of tall tales that also easily deceived the SEC staff investigators. There were six or seven SEC investigators in the room, one of them wearing a vest with the initials SEC on the back, like the vests worn by agents on law-enforcement raids.

Madoff was asked by the investigators if it was correct that all of the trades for his investment advisory clients were done by the London office.

"Yes," replied Madoff.

If the SEC staff had subpoenaed the records of the London office, it would have known this was a lie. But they did not question anyone in London, nor did they question Madoff's brother, Peter, or Bernie's sons, Mark and Andy, who were on the board of directors of the London office.

"Who are the counterparties to the options contracts?" the SEC lawyer asked.

"They're basically European banks," said Madoff, who was not asked to provide specific names or validating documents.

"Who has custody of the assets?" the SEC asked. "We do," said Madoff. It was a particularly bold lie because there were no assets. No stocks. No U.S. Treasury notes. Investigators have since found e-mails in which Madoff's right-hand man, Frank DiPascali, allegedly ordered the creation of documents showing that the assets were being held by Madoff.

"What is approximately the total amount of assets traded for these persons?" Madoff was asked.

"My guess would be something, a few hundred million dollars," replied Madoff. At the time, if his clients' monthly account statements had been added up, it would have indicated that the total amount of assets under management was in the tens of billions of dollars.

Madoff would later wonder "why didn't I get caught sooner?" In an interview in prison with Joe Cotchett, a lawyer planning to sue the Madoff family, Madoff said that this SEC session was the closest he came to getting caught.

Madoff told Cotchett that at one point, the SEC investigators said they wanted to see the actual stocks and securities held by Madoff.

"Where are they physically?" the SEC lead lawyer asked.

"With the Depository Trust Company," Madoff lied.

It was a Friday afternoon and Madoff told Cotchett that he expected he would be arrested by Monday after the SEC went to the Depository Trust Company and found that there were no stocks being held there for Madoff's investors. "I was sure they got me," Madoff said.

But the SEC lawyers never went to the Depository Trust Company, Madoff said. They took his word. At the time, in early 2006, Madoff estimated to Cotchett he had approximately $20 billion in U.S. Treasury notes. If true, and if he had been caught then, his victims would have had $20 billion to split up, instead of the $1 billion that was found after Madoff's arrest in 2008.

It was a hectic time for Madoff in 2006 and 2007 as he steered the SEC investigators away from the evidence that would have exposed his crimes. He did most of it without lawyers, who would have wanted to know the full story of what was happening on the seventeenth floor if they were expected to defend him.

Madoff did hire one prominent Washington law firm, WilmerHale, to deal with the issue of his failure to register as an investment adviser. Company records show Madoff paid WilmerHale $40,000 for its legal services in dealing with the SEC. The WilmerHale lawyer working for Madoff, Brandon Becker, has since left the firm and declined to comment. His name continued to be in Madoff's "little black book."

WilmerHale general counsel, Bruce Berman, said the firm dealt solely with the "narrow issue" of whether Madoff should register as an investment adviser. The SEC confirmed in a July 2006 letter that WilmerHale's representation was limited to the issue of registration, according to Berman. "He was careful in the way he used his lawyers," said Berman. Madoff billing records show that Madoff discussed his "market basket strategy" with the lawyers, but Berman said Madoff never gave them any reason to believe he was engaging in fraud.

"It is quite possible he lied to us in describing a trading strategy that didn't exist." Berman said the firm recommended that Madoff register as an investment adviser, and he did.

The SEC closed its investigation of Madoff on November 21, 2007. Over the course of twenty-three months, Madoff had pulled the strings like a master puppeteer, coaching Fairfield Greenwich, creating reams of phony documents, and lying through his teeth. It worked.

"The staff found no evidence of fraud," concluded the SEC in the Case Closing Recommendation filed by the Division of Enforcement. The SEC staff was somehow able to reconcile its finding with Madoff's earlier attempts to withhold information about customers' accounts and "mislead" (sic) its investigators about the nature of his trading strategy.

Branch chief Meaghan Cheung, who had expressed such contempt for Markopolos, signed off on the closing narrative along with the staff attorney who reported to her and the district administrator to whom she reported.

The SEC did find that Madoff had violated requirements that he register as an investment adviser. But that was a minor issue to the SEC, and it was resolved with "discussions" between Madoff and the staff that led Madoff to formally register as an investment adviser.

Madoff was pleasantly surprised when the SEC investigators closed the case after finding "no evidence of fraud." From Madoff's point of view, the incompetence of the SEC had once again kept him in business. Many of those same SEC investigators would be ordered back to the Madoff offices early on the morning of December 12. Madoff was under arrest in what the government was now calling the "world's biggest Ponzi scheme." Just as Markopolos had said so many times over so many years earlier.

"I recognized them from when they were here before," recalled Eleanor. "They had their heads down and had kind of that hangdog look."

"Clearly, the SEC failed as it has failed here in the past," said Massachusetts secretary of state Galvin. "If you were looking for a summary of why we have so many problems in our financial services sector, there it is."

Galvin, a Democrat, pointed to a culture in Washington during the Bill Clinton and George W. Bush administrations in which government tried to be "partners" with the industries it regulated. "The philosophy that was prevalent at the time, which was somehow government was in the way, we really didn't need any regulation, we were holding back our economy if we continued to do that, that was a fraud, too."

SEVEN

Eleanor

ELEANOR SQUILLARI ADORED BERNIE MADOFF IN EVERY WAY.

Even after the arrest, his secretary of twenty-five years was comfortable describing her feelings.

"I loved Bernie," she said in tears. "I did. I did."

Since the arrest and the revelation that he was a crook, however, she has come to feel a sense of betrayal and great anger. She is a woman scorned.

"I guess you could say he used me," she said with a sigh. "I knew a certain side of Bernie that I cared about. I thought he was a great guy."

Eleanor started working for Madoff in 1984, at the age of thirty-three. A tall, shapely, attractive brunette with an infectious laugh, she was a divorced mom raising a daughter and son.

"She was a looker," recalled Little Rick, the office messenger who was sometimes dispatched by Madoff to pick up marijuana in Spanish Harlem.

Eleanor started as the main receptionist when Bernard L. Madoff Investment Securities was still located at 110 Wall Street. Former employees say it was a place of fast-talking dealers and back-office workers who drank and partied hard, used lots of drugs, and liked to have sex on the boss's sofa with whomever they could find for the night.

After a brief stint working with the traders, Eleanor took over as the secretary for Bernie and his brother, Peter. "They were funny, they were smart. I thought they were good-looking and that they had their act together."

She also saw an intense sibling rivalry. "They fought all the time. Bernie would always set the rules and always had the last say. And Peter would follow."

Eleanor took great pride in her work. She made sure to be one of the first people in every morning, leaving her house on Staten Island at 5:40 a.m. to catch the X30 express bus or the ferry across the harbor for the hour-long trip to the office in Manhattan.

Like generations of women from Staten Island who have crossed the harbor every morning before dawn to work as secretaries for the city's powerful lawyers and financial titans, Eleanor was a power behind the throne at the Madoff firm. Her position as the boss's secretary meant she was the gatekeeper for anyone who needed time with Bernie. She ran his schedule, fielded the phone calls he didn't want to deal with, and kept his secrets—or at least the ones he chose to share with her. The "wild men" in the back office were careful about trying to hit on the boss's secretary.

Madoff could be a difficult boss, whose needling, crude jokes, and insulting comments were unrelenting. He would come out of the men's room with his zipper down, and when Eleanor rolled her eyes, "he would say 'Oh, come on, you know you want it.'" He wouldn't hesitate to tell her to "shut up" or suggest she was being paid too much.

In her early days there, she said, Bernie would feel free to pinch or pat the behinds of women in the office.

"In the beginning, I was much younger, and if he would be insulting, I would take it personally," recalled Eleanor. "He seemed to be somebody who liked to insult you." She is not a shy person and she soon felt comfortable enough to fire back. "'You know, you really shouldn't be talking to me like that.' He would pay attention to that and he would stop for maybe two weeks. And then he would go back to it."

They developed an easy, familiar relationship that allowed him to abuse her, with her tacit permission. "He knew that when he was under a lot of pressure he could yell at me, he could snap at me. When we were alone, I'd say, you know, you don't talk to people that way. We had that kind of relationship where he would listen." She knew there was no chance he would fire her. "He goes, I can't fire you; he goes, look how long you've been my secretary, people would believe you if you said something about me. So then I knew I could say whatever I wanted."

She was the office wife. Her salary was close to $80,000 a year, with a yearly bonus of almost $20,000. It was very good money for not a lot of work. Sometimes, Eleanor spent hours shopping online from her desk computer. When Bernie decided to cut off e-mails after the SEC asked questions about an e-mail from one Madoff employee, Eleanor successfully lobbied to have her connection restored. Increasingly, she was Bernie's eyes and ears when he spent weeks away in Florida or France. From her perch on the sleek nineteenth floor, in front of Bernie's glass-walled office, life looked very good to Eleanor, who learned to ignore Bernie's ugly side. "We thought we were working for this wonderful man. I loved my job and I loved the people that I worked with. And I was able to give my children everything that they needed."

There were always plenty of rumors around the office about Bernie's relationships with a long list of attractive women employees. They talked about the blonde on the seventeenth floor, and how Bernie was said to have paid for her apartment, where he visited her regularly. There was talk of a brunette, much younger than Bernie, who was abruptly dispatched to London. There was talk about his first secretary, Annette Bongiorno, who would become a multimillionaire and an alleged partner in his crimes. There were the escort service women and the professional masseuses. And there was even office gossip about Eleanor. She was included on two trips to ski resorts that Bernie organized for the staff. He gave her two photographic portraits of him to hang over her bed. "I did not hang them above my bed, that's for damn sure," said Eleanor. She stored the portraits in a closet. "I don't leave here thinking about you," she said she often reminded him. "So if he was under that illusion, I told him to get over it. And he said, 'Really?' and I said, 'Really.'"

"I'm not going there," she said when asked directly about rumors that she had an affair with Bernie. "There are much more important things to know about Bernie."

And since his arrest, no one has been more vocal or done more to make sure that everything else about Bernie, apart from the office gossip, is made known.

He stole from clients Eleanor came to know personally. He was ready to steal from her. "When my father passed away, I was a young single mom with two children. He took my money. He knew what he was doing. And you know, when he hired me he said, if you're loyal, he said, and you work hard, you'll go far. We'll take care of you. That was a lie. And I believed it."

Eleanor felt that even her presence outside his office for so many years had played a role in perpetuating

Bernie's fraud. "Part of the setup was that Bernie was able to say—and he loved to say—that 'Eleanor has been my secretary for twenty years. We don't have a big turnover; everybody here has been here forever.' Well that made the firm look very stable." She had no idea of the scam taking place two floors below her desk, on the seventeenth floor.

On the day of the arrest, she refused to believe her boss could have done anything illegal.

"Oh my God, you know, somebody's framing him. So I put a call in to his house, because he had to be there and I left a message and told him that I loved him."

It was when he called back twenty minutes later that she realized the painful truth. "I hung up the phone and I didn't want to admit it to anyone. I was still in the protective mode, I was still trying to protect him, and then I started to realize that this is what he had done. And I went home and I couldn't get out of bed Saturday because I knew. I knew."

Once she realized "he was a horrible person," she was heartbroken. "And then I started to get angry, I started to get really angry."

Anger and tears turned to action. She had to do something. Eleanor, essentially, opened her own investigation into her former boss. "I was looking at everything in a different light now." She wrote a first-person account of life as Bernie Madoff's secretary for *Vanity Fair*, which, according to someone at *Vanity Fair*, paid her at least $50,000. She made copies of every document she could find in the office and turned them over to the FBI. She recovered a two-foot-tall stack of documents copied directly from Madoff's filing cabinet and desk. These documents include spreadsheets, calendars, master phone lists, and legal bills.

"I was going to give it a shot because there had to be something in my files, in my drawers, anything. There had to be something. And I said, all right, here's a pattern. I did files on travel. I did files on calendars. I did files on people who may be of interest. I didn't know what I was doing, but I was doing it."

Among the most interesting documents Eleanor gave to the FBI was a copy of Madoff's expensive goatskin Hermès address book, the "little black book" that is a who's who of people Madoff considered his "most important contacts," with numbers for the office, home, and cell. After each name and number, Eleanor jotted down what she knew about the person and his or her relationship with Madoff.

In addition to the masseuses, escort service women, and the prominent SEC official already mentioned, there are dozens of other names that have provided important investigative leads to the FBI and other government agencies.

The first name listed is Annette Bongiorno, under A. Frank DiPascali is under D. David Friehling, Bernie's accountant at the strip mall in upstate New York, is listed. Bernie also included Dick Carroll, his longtime boat captain in Palm Beach, as well as the people who took care of his villa and yacht in France.

Many of his biggest clients—who were also his biggest victims—are in the book. These include Fred Wilpon, the owner of the New York Mets, who Eleanor says was much closer to the Madoff family than he has publicly acknowledged. Wilpon's son, Jeff, who now runs the Mets, was a close friend of Madoff's son Mark. Eleanor said that Mark arranged for one of Wilpon's girlfriends to work at the Madoff offices.

Also in the book are Swiss bankers, Spanish bankers, and British bankers. So are the so-called feeders and the hedge fund operators who billed huge fees for steering billions of dollars to Madoff with barely a second glance.

In addition to providing these documents, Eleanor's encyclopedic knowledge of names and numbers in the Madoff world and her memories of random events and meetings have provided other important leads to the FBI. "One thing the FBI said to me when we first started talking is, can you remember anything out of place or odd?"

For example, she recalls three different people who received regular cash payments from Madoff, in unmarked envelopes.

One of them, now deceased, lived in London, and Eleanor says she was often instructed to mail him a large stack of bills in U.S. currency. In an office that was regularly cutting checks and wiring hundreds of millions of dollars to people around the world, this person received his payments in cash. "I look at it now and I go, oh my God. I was really stupid, but I didn't think about it."

The two other cash recipients picked up their payments from Eleanor in person at the Madoff offices. One of them was an elderly woman who Eleanor believes was an eccentric client who "had a thing" about getting cash. The other person, however, had Eleanor's investigative instincts working overtime. He received regular cash payments stuffed into a white envelope. She has provided his name to the FBI and describes him as someone very close to Madoff who is connected to a major Wall Street brokerage firm. The person and his wife remain close to Ruth Madoff. Was he in on the scheme? Was he a bagman paying off a corrupt official? Or was he just another client with an idiosyncratic need for cash instead of a check? Eleanor does not know, but she wants anyone involved in Madoff's scam, even onetime friends, to get caught and pay a price.

"People made the wrong choices. They're gonna be made examples of. It is very unfortunate. They all have families."

In the days after Bernie's arrest and the exposure of his Ponzi scheme, Eleanor says she was traumatized from handling the phone calls of cheated investors.

"I'm haunted by these people. I don't sleep well. I'm just haunted by it, I can't get over it. It was all the voices that I heard. I always used to get phone calls; gee, do you think Bernie will consider having, you know, my brother-in-law come in, or my neighbor, or this one or that one. So not only did they lose their money, now they have to live with the guilt of bringing in all the people they cared about."

As the encyclopedia of Madoff, Eleanor was relied on heavily by the FBI to figure out who was who and how they were related. She knew the family tree, and she continued to report to work every day until March, when she told the agents she was being paid by *Vanity Fair* for her story. She was told she could no longer stay in the office, but the agents continued to call her with questions.

Other than Bernie and Ruth, Eleanor has become the best known figure in the Madoff scandal. She has received praise from many of her former colleagues for speaking out, including from Madoff's son Andy, who told her he thought she had written a good article.

Having watched them come of age, she believes that Andy and his older brother, Mark, could not have been involved in the Ponzi scheme. "I was there for twenty-five years and I think I would've at some point seen them involved in some way. Even in a conversation. I never did. I would find it hard to believe that they would wait for me to take a day off or go on vacation to openly participate. It just didn't happen. Nobody is that good an actor for twenty-five years—other than their father."

Bernard Madoff's portraits have long since been taken

out of the closet in Eleanor's apartment and given away or put up for sale. Yet she admits she still cares about the man with whom she shared so much for so long.

"I still have feelings for him because I haven't reconciled the fact that there was this horrible side to him, this side that I think snowballed, it evolved, he got used to it, he got comfortable with it, and then he just went wild with it. We thought we were doing the right thing for our families. And we just thought that we were having a nice life. And we weren't."

EIGHT

The Men Who Should Have Known

WALTER NOEL APPEARED TO HAVE IT ALL. AS A RESULT, HE was despised by many in his hometown of Greenwich, Connecticut.

Status and wealth are closely tracked in this elite New York suburb. His envious neighbors found the courtly seventy-nine-year-old "affable enough," with his gentle Tennessee accent and manners. But given his seemingly ordinary grasp of finances and the market, they could not understand how he had been able to achieve a level of wealth that was remarkable even by Greenwich standards.

"I had lunch with him several times and he just wasn't that smart," said one prominent hedge fund owner whose own earnings and track record could not match Noel's.

What the hedge fund owner did not know was that Noel had been able to achieve record investment returns and become very rich because he was one of Bernie Madoff's "feeders." Since 1989, he had made hundreds of millions of dollars in huge commissions on the money that, for the most part, he simply sent from his clients to Madoff's secretive operation.

The "mechanics" who had produced the phony statements and created the fictitious trades on the seventeenth floor of Madoff's New York offices were an essential ingredient of the scheme, but their work wouldn't have amounted to much without the "money men" like Noel. These were the men who trolled the country clubs and the suburbs and the exclusive resorts, recruiting wealthy clients for Madoff. There were dozens of them, but none more important than Noel and his firm, Fairfield Greenwich, whose clients comprised the single biggest account in Madoff's empire. When Madoff was arrested, Noel's clients thought they had $7.2 billion invested with Madoff. In fact, they had nothing.

Noel's lifestyle and social prominence had grown in tandem with Madoff's scam. He and his Brazilian-born wife, Monica, had a huge mansion on Greenwich's prestigious Round Hill Road. They owned an oceanfront estate on Long Island, in Southampton. For those nights when the black-tie charity balls went too late, there was a New York apartment on Park Avenue. The crown jewel in the

Noel empire, however, was a hilltop villa on the privately owned Caribbean island of Mustique.

According to a profile of the Noels that appeared in *Town & Country*, their villa had its own name, Yemanjá, the Brazilian goddess of the sea. His Round Hill neighbors in Greenwich who thought they were so much smarter had a serious case of envy as they flipped through the glossy pages of the magazine and read about the great Walter Noel and his island retreat.

His wife "shopped uptown Manhattan" for fabrics and "downtown at an African importer" for wooden stools and benches. Monica was "indefatigable, she scoped out the furniture market in High Point, North Carolina, and the designer showrooms in Dania, Florida, for bamboo side tables, dining chairs, and ceramics." Top-name architects, designers, and landscapers were flown in as Monica created "just the insouciant, global primitive style she was after." Tommy Hilfiger said the Noels had "the best view on the island."

A photo spread with the *Town & Country* piece showed handsome Walter embracing the statuesque Monica, both smiling broadly. Most important, their five grown daughters loved the Mustique house and the way it was decorated. The women, all slim and beautiful enough to be fashion models, were pictured at Yemanjá, seated on large cushions covered with yards of that expensive uptown fabric. They were so proud that their parents were hip. "I mean, our houses in New York and Greenwich are very nice," daughter Marisa told *Town & Country*, "but they're polite—it wasn't the sexy chic feeling this place needed."

The *Town & Country* article was published in May 2005, just six months before Fairfield Greenwich would play a key role in what the SEC called "Madoff's shell game" to deceive federal regulators about his scam. Its chief risk officer had been coached by Madoff about how to best answer questions posed by SEC investigators. Fairfield Greenwich was sued by the Madoff bankruptcy trustee and virtually every client it had for failing to do the sort of extensive background checks and "due diligence" on Madoff that it promised it would do.

In 2012, Fairfield Greenwich agreed to an $80 million settlement of a class action lawsuit brought by investors. The downfall of Bernie Madoff meant the downfall of Walter Noel and the dozens of other prominent "money men" or "feeders" who, wittingly or not, kept the Ponzi scheme going. The lawsuits allege that they "knew or should have known." They have all claimed they were unaware of the scam.

In addition to Noel, the feeders included a long list of supposedly savvy individuals, including Ezra Merkin of New York and Stanley Chais of Los Angeles. Merkin was a longtime friend of Madoff and served on the board of trustees of Yeshiva University with him. Merkin began investing clients' money with Madoff in 1995 through his

Ascot, Gabriel Capital, and Ariel funds. He had only four months of negative returns out of one hundred months through 2008.

"Returns this good could not be reproduced by other skilled hedge fund managers," alleged the bankruptcy trustee overseeing Madoff's business. New York attorney general Andrew Cuomo charged that "Merkin betrayed hundreds of investors who entrusted him with their savings by recklessly feeding their funds into the largest Ponzi scheme in history, while falsely claiming he actively managed their funds."

Merkin took the position that he "had performed extensive due diligence," and if Madoff had been able to fool federal regulators, how could anyone blame Merkin for being fooled, too? But the New York attorney general said Merkin had been warned again and again that Madoff was a fraud, but he would nevertheless eventually steer more than $2 billion to Madoff. Much of it came from Jewish charities and schools, including Yeshiva University. They lost a large part of their endowment because of what the attorney general called "Merkin's deceit, recklessness." Merkin's lawyers promised a vigorous defense in court. In April, 2013 he settled with the New York Attorney General for $410 million.

Similar allegations were made against Stanley Chais and the investment funds he represented. In a court filing, the bankruptcy trustee said, "Despite having clear indications that Madoff was conducting a fraud, Chais persisted" and collected "over $250 million in fees for his purported 'services.'" Chais's clients, who included a number of movie-industry figures, thought they had $900 million in assets when the Madoff scam was exposed. They had, in fact, nothing.

Chais's attorneys claim he was "blindsided and victimized" by Madoff. "Mr. Chais and his family have lost virtually everything—an impossible result were he involved in the underlying fraud," Chais's lawyers Eugene Licker and Amanda Merkur said.

Over the years, Madoff's savvy investors became convinced that he had his own foolproof system, which some thought might not be completely aboveboard, but which could, bottom line, keep those big returns coming. They believed that if Madoff got caught, it would be his problem—not theirs.

Their greed led them to miss some very obvious warning signs.

"It was a great con. The best cons are when you keep the pigeons happy, right? And the pigeons were happy because they were getting good returns," said investment adviser Suzanne Murphy.

Walter Noel was a very happy pigeon for a long time. He was introduced to Madoff in 1989 by the father-in-law of his partner, Jeffrey Tucker. Noel and Tucker started by giving Madoff $1.5 million to invest from an investment fund they had created. They called it a "test" investment. Six months later they sent Madoff another million dollars, then $4 million, then hundreds of millions. Not only were his steady year-to-year returns of 12 to 20 percent thrilling the clients of Fairfield Greenwich, Noel and his partner Tucker were also getting rich.

Unlike almost any other hedge fund in the history of Wall Street, Madoff did not charge Noel and Tucker's firm anything to invest all that money. As a result, they could pocket all of the standard hedge fund fees. This amounted to 1 or 2 percent of the total money invested and 20 percent of any profit, "one and twenty" or "two and twenty" in the parlance of Wall Street. All theirs. They did not have to share with Bernie.

"If you're Walter Noel, you ask the question, why is Bernie Madoff letting me make all this money?" said Suzanne Murphy. "It just doesn't make sense. They were not making the trades, they were not making any investment decisions. All they were doing was collecting the money."

Noel and Tucker's firm earned $100 million a year for doing virtually nothing. Ninety-nine percent of the money in their Sentry Fund was invested with Madoff. It was an amazing deal. Over the years, Madoff left hundreds of millions of dollars on the table for Noel and Tucker to scoop up for themselves. The homes in Greenwich, Southampton, Manhattan, and Mustique were easily affordable, along with the private jets and all the other trappings of a successful hedge fund operator.

It was the same arrangement Madoff had with all of

his other feeder funds. He claimed he made his money
by charging 4 cents for every share of stock he traded on
their behalf and $1 for each option contract. This was
a complete lie, as no shares were ever traded, or option
contracts purchased.

It's not known if Walter Noel ever questioned why
Madoff was forgoing so much profit, but he clearly
believed he had found the golden goose in Bernie. To
expand his empire and bring in even larger profits, Noel
enlisted the help of his gorgeous daughters, or at least
their husbands. Four of his five sons-in-law joined him
in the business, setting up offices in Europe and South
America to recruit new investors whose money could be
steered to Madoff, so Fairfield Greenwich could collect
their extravagant fees. According to Massachusetts secretary of state William Galvin, one of Noel's sons-in-law
and his partner, Andres Piedrahita, a Colombian who
operated out of Madrid, earned more than $45 million in
2008 alone.

Noel and Tucker and the sons-in-law told their clients they deserved their large fees because they could
guarantee access to Madoff and make sure it was a safe
investment that no one had to worry about. According
to Galvin, they completely disregarded their duties. "Its
flagrant and recurring misrepresentations to its investors
rises to the level of fraud," he charged.

In a stack of documents and e-mails recording Fairfield Greenwich's behavior, none is more damning than

the glossy brochure sent to its clients to describe the company's "due diligence." The brochure said that the fund may "reject an otherwise appealing manager" if it detected an "operational risk," including "misrepresentation of valuations and outright fraud." Fairfield Greenwich claimed it "verifies assets under management for all funds directly" and "provides independent, third party confirmation of assets." In other words, the fund knew Bernie Madoff had traded all of those stocks he claimed to have traded, because it had independent confirmation.

The statement was not even close to true, according to investigators. Fairfield Greenwich agreed to let Madoff be both the custodian of the stocks and the broker that executed the trade. Their verification consisted of checking Madoff's brokerage records against Madoff's asset holding records. Of course, since both were created by the same team, they always matched perfectly. There was no independent third party. This was Ponzi Scheme Protection 101.

A few Fairfield Greenwich executives had toured Madoff's offices, but no one had ever seen the seventeenth floor, where all of the trades were supposedly being directed. The only person other than Madoff whom the Fairfield Greenwich executives had met or could name was Frank DiPascali, Madoff's seventeenth-floor crew boss. He met them upstairs, away from the secret rooms. DiPascali wore a suit and a tie on those days, according to former employees, apparently aware of the importance of making a good impression on the firm's single biggest sucker.

Fairfield Greenwich's faith in Madoff was largely based on what can best be described as a magic show that Madoff and DiPascali put on for them in 2001. Madoff had asked Tucker to visit the offices after a critical article about Madoff appeared in the finance magazine *Barron's*, titled "Don't Ask, Don't Tell." The magician, Madoff, and his assistant, DiPascali, set out to prove *Barron's* was wrong. They were not frauds. They had all the stocks they said they had. Tucker was instructed to open a journal that Madoff said had all of the stocks held by Madoff Securities. Tucker was asked "Pick any two stocks." Pick a card, pick any card.

Tucker picked AOL Time Warner and in the journal he saw the number of shares in that company that Madoff held on behalf of Fairfield Greenwich. Now, with a wave of his wand, Madoff had Frank activate a computer screen that Tucker was told was from the Depository Trust Company, a major Wall Street clearinghouse that holds stocks for customers. The magician's assistant scrolled through the pages until he got to AOL/Time Warner and Fairfield Greenwich. Presto! Abracadabra! The number on the screen and the number in the Madoff ledger matched perfectly. The trick worked on Tucker. He was convinced. There was no need to pick a second stock.

"I knew of my own that the position I saw for us was roughly what we had because I was somewhat familiar with our size, you know, in shares," Tucker later said. "That was basically the meeting." The magic show was over, and Tucker drove back to Greenwich, relieved and unaware that he had been fooled by the Amazing Madoff's command performances. Madoff had created phony ledgers and, with DiPascali's help, a bogus computer page for the Depository Trust Company, the DTC. Asked later by investigators how he knew it was the DTC screen he had been looking at, Tucker said, "It had a logo. It had a DTC logo."

Had he ever seen a DTC screen before? "No."

"And because he was telling you that—because Madoff told you that—"

"Yeah, of course."

"Have you ever seen a DTC screen since then?"

"No."

"And did you get a printout of the DTC screen?"

"No."

"Did you repeat that review with any other equity or option, or was it just the AOL shares?"

"I think just the AOL."

Once was enough. There was no need for any more of Madoff's magic.

Over the years, as clients raised a number of questions about Madoff, Fairfield Greenwich repeatedly gave them short shrift. They thought they had seen the proof, and they were reassured when, over the years, Madoff was able to honor some $3 billion in redemption requests.

In 2005, one of Fairfield Greenwich's Sentry Fund customers asked a pointed question about Madoff's accountant, Friehling & Horowitz. "Bernard L. Madoff Securities LLC has employed a small accounting firm," the customer wrote. "Is that accounting firm checked and approved by Fairfield Greenwich Group?" As noted earlier, Friehling & Horowitz was a three-person operation working out of a strip mall in a small town north of New York City. No one at Fairfield Greenwich had ever spoken to Friehling, the lead accountant, or done any background checks on him until the customer's inquiry.

Fairfield's chief financial officer, Dan Lipton, picked up the phone and called the Friehling offices. He does not remember the name of the "partner" he talked with, but it must have been Friehling because he was the only full-time partner at Friehling & Horowitz. Horowitz, Friehling's father-in-law, was in retirement in Florida. Lipton recalls he was told the firm had "hundreds of clients" and was "well respected in the community."

Other than checking on the Internet to see that the firm was in good standing with its certified public accounting license and was a member of the local chapters of the CPA, Lipton made no effort to corroborate what Friehling told him. Fairfield's chief risk officer also was satisfied that Friehling & Horowitz were independent auditors, because, he later testified, "on the front of the report it said 'independent auditor.'"

No one ever traveled to New York's Rockland County to inspect the office. If they had, they would have discovered that it was an eighteen-by-thirteen-foot space. The firm's total revenues were $180,000, hardly in keeping with the fees that would have been earned by conducting a full, independent audit of a $65 billion hedge fund.

Nevertheless, Fairfield Greenwich assured its anxious customer that there was no problem with the accountant. Based on a statement provided by his chief financial officer, Lipton, Jeff Tucker wrote to his suspicious client on September 12, 2005, that "Friehling & Horowitz CPAs are a small- to medium-sized financial services audit and tax firm specializing in broker/dealers and other financial services firms. . . .

They have hundreds of clients and are well-respected in the local community," Tucker said, passing on as truth the lies Friehling had told to cover for Bernie Madoff.

Two days later, Tucker, Lipton, and the firm's general counsel, Mark McKeefrey, received a disturbing e-mail from Gordon McKenzie, the Fairfield controller. He had done some more checking on Friehling & Horowitz and reported, "It appears Friehling is the only employee." So how could they have hundreds of clients in the financial services industry? One accountant could never handle such a workload. Tucker's only response to the e-mail was, "Thank you." Fairfield Greenwich took no further steps to answer some very obvious discrepancies and questions.

They continued to cite the Friehling & Horowitz audits as proof that Madoff was indeed all he said he was.

An SEC investigation of Madoff was launched only a few months after Fairfield Greenwich had dealt with the questions about the accountant. Now there were allegations that Madoff might be running a Ponzi scheme, and SEC investigators considered Fairfield Greenwich an important source of information. As Madoff's single biggest customer, Fairfield Greenwich, with its "robust due diligence," would certainly know if there was anything to be concerned about.

But the fact was that Fairfield Greenwich knew very little about Madoff. That ignorance would have become very troubling for them if it became known to the SEC. It also could have been a violation of securities law to promise clients "due diligence" and then not perform it. So Fairfield Greenwich had plenty of reasons to allow its chief risk officer, Amit Vijayvergiya, to be "briefed" by Madoff on what to say to the SEC.

Noel's partner Jeff Tucker was also "voluntarily" interviewed by the SEC. Fairfield Greenwich gave Madoff high marks. In the view of the Massachusetts secretary of state, Madoff's ability to coach the witness "likely helped him evade SEC detection."

In the second half of 2008, when the financial system and the market were on the edge of collapse, a number of Fairfield Greenwich clients wanted to take money out of

Madoff's company. Some needed the money to make up margin calls and losses elsewhere. Others began to have concerns about Madoff himself.

Fairfield Greenwich tried to stop the withdrawals. The chief risk officer, Vijayvergiya, also had a role in marketing Madoff to Sentry Fund clients. He was working on a plan to persuade Fairfield Greenwich customers not to withdraw their money from Madoff. One of the firm's partners, David Horn, the chief global strategist, warned him about a prospective client who was considering an investment of $50 million to $100 million. "She has heard about Madoff but hears things that scare her," read the e-mail Vijayvergiya received. "So neutralize the scare with our transparency. This will be a piece of cake," Horn wrote.

Yet the withdrawals and concerns continued. There had been discussion and serious concern inside Fairfield Greenwich that Madoff would "blow up."

As the markets dried up, how did Madoff continue to do so well? Who was buying and selling him the options that were critical to his "split strike conversion" strategy that no one else really understood? Nobody else was able to do what Madoff said he was doing in this tight market. DiPascali had told them about "twenty derivatives dealers and international banks, primarily European," who were the "counterparties," but he would not provide specific names. Only Bernie could reveal those secrets.

Vijayvergiya had a meeting scheduled with Madoff on October 2. "If anyone feels we should urgently contact Bernie in advance of this meeting, we can do so," he wrote.

Although its customers had no idea there was any concern about Madoff, Fairfield Greenwich was beginning to feel the twinges of panic. When some of its clients raised the same questions it had about who was buying and selling Madoff's vital options and puts, the "counterparties," Fairfield Greenwich answered, "We do not give out the names of the counterparties used [,] but they are all well established financial institutions. All counterparties are rated A or better and they are not affiliated with Madoff." In fact, Fairfield Greenwich still had no idea who Madoff used as counterparties. Madoff would not tell them because the truth was that there were no counterparties. If he had made up names, they could have been too easily checked.

Fairfield Greenwich made another feeble attempt at due diligence in Madoff's office at the October 2 meeting. Walter Noel and Jeff Tucker attended, as did their general counsel, Mark McKeefrey. Vijayvergiya was on the phone, listening. Madoff had been given a list of "priority" questions to close some of the "gaps" in Fairfield Greenwich's knowledge of his operation. After nineteen years in which they had invested billions of dollars with Madoff, Noel and Tucker still had barely a clue of what Madoff was doing to earn such huge returns.

Yet Madoff continued to dodge and hedge on the written questionnaire. "Please provide a list of key personnel involved in the split strike conversion strategy. Provide a description of their roles." Madoff answered, "The people involved in the SSC (split strike conversation) strategy are traders, analysts, programmers, and operations people. No names given."

The evasions were getting more obvious, yet no one at the meeting pushed for answers. When he was again asked for the names of the counterparties, Madoff's response, recorded in the meeting notes, was "BLM will not disclose the names of the c/p's 'for obvious reasons' (i.e. confidentiality)." Vijayvergiya later told investigators from the Massachusetts secretary of state's office, "I don't recall if anyone at this meeting pushed back and asked for a specific response."

Madoff had always played hard to get with his investors, even with Fairfield Greenwich. In October 2008, however, he abruptly reversed his "long-standing policy" of limiting how much money Fairfield Greenwich could put into his firm. In fact, he showed flashes of anger when informed of the growing number of Fairfield Greenwich clients who wanted to pull their money out. Madoff had dropped the "hard-to-get" pose.

Fairfield Greenwich came to his defense, passing on tales such as the assurances about the mystery counterparties that they later admitted to investigators they knew nothing about. Vijayvergiya also sent investors a notice that as of mid-September, Madoff had put all of the money into safe U.S. Treasury notes. Madoff, the genius, was out of the market. It seemed he had once again predicted the future and acted accordingly.

Remarkably, Madoff told Fairfield Greenwich that one of his cash holdings was with the Fidelity Spartan U.S. Treasury Money Market Fund. The Fidelity Spartan Fund no longer existed. It had been renamed the Fidelity Fund in 2005. No one noticed Madoff's error.

Still, with the market in crisis and questions about Madoff swirling, the redemptions from Fairfield Greenwich clients continued and Madoff was uncharacteristically furious. Mr. Cool was no longer so calm and uncaring. He was no longer playing hard to get. He scolded and berated Jeff Tucker and threatened to cut him off. It was December 8, three days before Madoff's arrest. "Just got off the phone with a very angry Bernie, who said if we can't replace the redemptions for 12/31 he is going to close the account," Tucker reported to the firm's executive committee and Walter Noel.

The golden goose was making threats. "His traders are 'tired of dealing with these hedge funds' and there are plenty of institutions who can replace the money. They have been offered this all along but 'remained loyal to us,'" Tucker wrote of his conversation. Madoff was bluffing, but Tucker believed him. "I think he is sincere," he wrote.

Fairfield set up new funds in the last months of 2008 to try to pump additional money into Madoff's operation. "We tried to help stem things," Noel said. "We thought, well, we can help him a bit if we give him some more money." They raised almost $15 million for what was called the Greenwich Emerald Fund, which the Massachusetts secretary of state said was formed without any of the legally required offering documents. There was no time to waste if the angry Madoff had to be appeased. Fairfield Greenwich was desperate. The small amount in the Sentry Fund that was not already invested with Madoff was also sent his way. Several hundred million dollars from other funds was sent to Madoff as well, and the firm covered another $150 million in client redemptions by taking over their investments with Madoff. Tucker and his wife had invested some of their own money in one of the new funds, as a vote of confidence and because he believed it was a "good investment." Noel and Tucker pushed hard.

On December 10, the day Madoff would admit to his sons that he was a fraud, Tucker wrote a letter to Madoff detailing all the steps Fairfield Greenwich was taking to avoid being cut off from the huge fees they had earned over the years. On the morning of December 11, the day Madoff was arrested, Vijayvergiya was still pushing investments to Madoff and marketing the "superior due diligence" that had been conducted on him. The news of the arrest came only a few hours later.

People at Fairfield Greenwich immediately understood that they were in serious trouble. The chief financial officer, Lipton, sent an e-mail trying to shift his personal assets out of his name. "My wife needs to open a brokerage account today in only her name. And I would like to transfer my munis and Treasuries into it." Elsewhere, one of Fairfield Greenwich's account executives in London also sensed big trouble. It was obvious that lots of questions were going to be asked about who knew what when. And the London executive desperately sought any paperwork that could be used as proof that he had confirmed Madoff's supposed trades for a Fairfield Greenwich fund called Sigma that had sent money to Madoff. "In order to cover my ass, can I get some copies of those trades? I need to show to people who invested in Sigma that I was doing due diligence in what is the largest scam in financial history."

NINE

The Victims

TWELVE DAYS AFTER BERNARD MADOFF ADMITTED TO THE FBI that he had cheated thousands of people out of billions of dollars, one of his victims committed suicide.

Rene-Thierry Magon de la Villehuchet, a sixty-five-year-old French aristocrat who lived and worked in New York as an investment adviser for Access International Advisors, was found dead in his office in Manhattan on December 23. He had taken sleeping pills and then slit his wrists.

Madoff was at the kitchen table of his penthouse apartment, under luxurious house arrest, when he learned of the suicide. He sneered.

"That guy couldn't pick a stock if his life depended on

it," Madoff said to a stunned visitor about the dead Mr. de la Villehuchet.

There was no emotion, no regret that his crimes had led to a death, the visitor said. Only contempt for a man whom Madoff dismissed as unable to pick a stock. Of course, Madoff's own legendary ability to pick stocks was based on cheating. His fraud scheme depended on picking stocks after the market had closed, when he already knew the winners and losers. Madoff never actually traded any stocks for his investors, and his picks were just a fiction to persuade his investors that they were making huge returns.

De la Villehuchet, the gentlemanly French financial adviser, had invested $1.4 billion of his and his clients' money with Madoff over the years because of Madoff's supposed brilliance with the market. In the weeks before the arrest, executives from de la Villehuchet's investment firm had met with Madoff. The independent fraud investigator, Harry Markopolos, apparently had tried to warn de la Villehuchet's firm but said that their risk manager "refused to meet with me to discuss my proof that Bernie was a fraud." De la Villehuchet had lost his life savings in the Ponzi scheme, but worried more about what he had done to his clients. "He felt, as we say in French, guilty but not responsible," said his brother, Bertrand.

Madoff felt neither guilt nor responsibility.

"Madoff wouldn't understand the reaction of my

brother. It was his honor, a word that's not in his [Madoff's] vocabulary," said Bertrand de la Villehuchet.

According to former FBI agent Brad Garrett, Madoff's reaction to the suicide of one of his victims was a classic manifestation of an antisocial personality. "An antisocial personality basically is a person with no conscience," said Garrett. "I call them boomerang personalities. Everything I throw at you, you throw back at me. It's always the other person's fault." In the case of de la Villehuchet, Madoff blamed the Frenchman. "He's weak, he committed suicide," Garrett imagined Madoff thinking.

Garrett knows Madoff's type well from dealing with serial killers and other criminals. "They are just monsters to deal with because they will not accept responsibility. If they admit anything, they're going to make some comment about how that person had it coming to them. 'They wouldn't be shit without me.'"

Police call Ponzi schemes affinity scams because they almost always involve groups of people who know one another. Madoff's victims all knew someone who knew someone who knew Bernie. Madoff did not have to put advertisements in the *Wall Street Journal* to recruit clients. Given his reputation for steady returns of 12 to 20 percent, customers were banging on the door to get in.

"We felt like we were the luckiest people in the world because we certainly weren't millionaires," said Laura Stein, a nutrition specialist who wrote *The Bloomingdale's*

Eat Healthy Diet book. "We thought he would never bother with small potatoes like us."

When the market collapsed in the fall of 2008, Stein and her husband moved all of their other investments into the Madoff account because he continued to make profits—or so their monthly statements indicated.

"Our accountant called and spoke to my husband," Laura said, "who walked up the stairs very slowly and he said, 'I have very bad news.' And I thought someone had died and then he said Bernie Madoff had been arrested." They lost everything.

On December 11, 2008, thousands of people received similarly bad news. Madoff's actual number of accounts totaled only 4,903, but many of the accounts belonged to investment firms or hedge funds, the "feeders," who had invested money on behalf of their own set of clients.

The early headlines focused on the well-known names that showed up on Madoff's victim list. The acting couple of Kevin Bacon and Kyra Sedgwick were among the famous losers. Director Steven Spielberg and Dream-Works executive Jeffrey Katzenberg, steered to Madoff by famed Hollywood accountant Gerald Breslauer, had invested money with Madoff for their charitable foundations. Oscar-winning screenwriter Eric Roth lost several million dollars as he was celebrating the opening of his latest film, *The Curious Case of Benjamin Button*. While their losses were large, the A-list victims did not face the loss of their homes or imminent bankruptcy like so many others who had invested with Madoff but did not have names that get boldface type in the papers.

"I heard about Spielberg and those people, naturally. It's a write-off for them. But for us, ten million is a lot," said the husband of Zsa Zsa Gabor, the ninety-eight-year-old actress whose A-list, gossip column days were long over.

Zsa Zsa and her husband, Frédéric Prinz von Anhalt, lost their life savings when the Madoff scheme collapsed. They feared they might lose their Bel Air mansion (they were ultimately were able to keep it), their two Rolls-Royce sedans, and—most important of all—what was left of their dignity.

"At her age, you know, she's very upset. She nearly had a heart attack when she found out," said von Anhalt in a European accent that matched his wife's famous Hungarian lilt. They had put their money in Madoff through a Los Angeles investment fund and did not immediately realize they were victims of the Ponzi scheme. Once Zsa Zsa understood what had happened, she blamed her husband. "So now my wife is furious and I have sleepless nights because every evening I go to bed, my wife stalks about: 'What happened, what happened?' It's terrible. It's a disaster for us."

As von Anhalt was being interviewed on the first floor of the mansion, Zsa Zsa was upstairs in her bedroom. She has been confined to a wheelchair since suffering an auto accident in 2002 and a stroke in 2005. She would not show her face with the cameras present, but she could be heard shouting at her guilt-ridden husband, still angry about the loss.

"It didn't happen to Zsa Zsa Gabor, it happened to me, because my wife trusted me," said von Anhalt. "It's enough to kill myself, but I'm not going to do it. I'm not doing him the favor. I want my money back. I want to squeeze the bastard. I want him to go down. And I want to see him going down. That is going to satisfy me."

Only a few of Madoff's victims had Bel Air mansions, but the personal recriminations and anger and fear that Zsa Zsa and her husband were going through were scenes that played out at kitchen tables around the country and all around the world in homes of all sizes. "It's your fault. How could you have trusted him?" Like Zsa Zsa, Madoff's elderly victims no longer had the ability to go back into the job market and make a living. They had counted on him to get them through retirement. Everything was gone. One ninety-year-old investor was told by her nursing home she would have to leave because she no longer had the ability to pay.

Others counted on the money they had with Madoff to pay for their children's college education or for pressing medical needs. Behind every Madoff account number was a heartbreaking story and a crippling sense of betrayal.

"There are going to be suicides, there is going to be divorce and upheaval," said psychotherapist Heath King, whose clients include several Madoff victims. "It can be devastating not only financially but mentally and emotionally. There will be a lot of accusations and counter-accusations that will create more of a fissure in relationships that were based on image and money in the first place."

As such, Palm Beach, Florida, was especially hard hit. With its exclusive clubs, expensive shops, trophy wives, and multimillion-dollar mansions hidden behind tall hedges, the tiny island is an enclave of the wealthy. It's a place that's all about image and money.

"Palm Beach is a prototype of what F. Scott Fitzgerald referred to when he said that the wealthy have problems that the poor know not of," said psychotherapist King, who sees many patients from Palm Beach.

Bernie and Ruth Madoff were among Palm Beach's most prominent residents, and many of Madoff's victims were fellow members of the Palm Beach Country Club. The Palm Beach Country Club was founded in the 1950s by a group of wealthy men who could not get into the city's other prominent clubs because they were Jewish. Madoff listed two of his biggest recruiters, Robert Jaffe and Sonny Cohn of Cohmad, as personal references in his membership application.

Club members vied to have Madoff take them on as investment advisory clients. Many of them sought recommendations from someone who was already lucky enough to be one of Madoff's clients. Madoff was above it all. His marketing strategy was to play hard to get. "He cultivated an aura of success and secrecy," the SEC found, "shunning one-on-one meetings with most individual investors and arbitrarily refusing prospective investors for what appeared to be whimsical or snobbish reasons."

Hundreds of the country-club set found a connection to Bernie through fellow member Robert Jaffe, another member of the club, whose wife, Ellen, was the daughter of Carl Shapiro, one of Madoff's first and biggest clients. His father-in-law's longtime connection to Madoff helped Jaffe get the job in the first place.

Jaffe is a debonair former clothing salesman from Boston with a perpetual tan, who could usually be found at the club or driving around town in his Jaguar convertible. He had a mansion just down the street from Bernie's that was even bigger and grander than Madoff's. He was well known for his ability to make an introduction or "put in a good word" to Bernie. "He was perceived to be a door opener to Madoff," said William Galvin, the Massachusetts secretary of state.

Unbeknownst to many, Jaffe was being paid by Madoff to steer customers and their money to him. He had been hired to work at what investigators called a "front" for Madoff. The company, Cohmad, was part-owned by Madoff and used, essentially, as Madoff's secret sales force. According to investigators, Cohmad conducted no business on its own other than to transfer money to Madoff. This was part of what the SEC later called Madoff's "shell game" to deceive regulators.

Jaffe took the Fifth Amendment when he was questioned by the Securities and Exchange Commission and Massachusetts secretary of state William Galvin about Cohmad and Madoff. "The amount of fees that Mr. Jaffe made as a result of his interaction with Mr. Madoff has certainly raised some serious questions," said Galvin. Jaffe's payments from Madoff were deposited directly in his Madoff account, supposedly accruing interest of up to 46 percent per year. In the last twelve years, he took out more than $150 million. When the scheme collapsed, Jaffe was wiped out, according to the public relations person he later hired. Even Madoff's salespeople were victims in a certain respect.

Jaffe was not willing to speak about his role in Madoff's fraud. When an ABC News producer sought to take his picture outside the crowded Bice restaurant in Palm Beach one evening, Jaffe grabbed the camera out of her hands and smashed it onto the concrete pavement. His spokesman said, "He got a little emotional." The spokesman said Jaffe "never, ever misled anyone" and that he, too, along with his father-in-law, Shapiro, were victims of Madoff.

"We recognize that he's a piece of the puzzle," said Galvin as he began his investigation. "He obviously could have provided us with a lot more information about how the Madoff empire worked. He declined to do so."

In June, 2009, the SEC charged Jaffe and Cohmad with civil fraud, alleging that they "knew or should have known" that they were working for a Ponzi scheme. In a statement, Jaffe's lawyer, Stanley Arkin, said the SEC action "smacks of impulsiveness and efforts at self-justification. It is unfair, baseless in the law, and is inaccurate in its understanding of the facts and of Mr. Jaffe."

In a settlement with the SEC in November, 2010, Jaffe was barred from association with any broker, dealer, or investment adviser. In a separate settlement with the trustee, Jaffe agreed to turn over $38 million. Jaffe neither admitted nor denied the allegations against him, according to the SEC documents.

With Jaffe's help, Madoff collected more than a billion dollars from the elite of the Palm Beach Jewish community. When his crime was exposed, they were stunned to learn that Madoff, their nine-handicap golf partner and charming dinner guest, was an outright crook.

"He was stealing from his own crowd," said psychotherapist King. "There is this sense of betrayal. And with betrayal comes anger."

After Madoff was safely under house arrest, Jaffe continued to be out and about at the finest restaurants and clubs in Palm Beach. For some, it was too much when he showed up at the grand ballroom of Donald Trump's country club, Mar-a-Lago, for a society birthday party.

"Unfortunately about forty percent of the people at the party had been ripped off by Madoff," said Trump, who was also there that night. "When he walked in the door there were a lot of angry eyes, blood pouring out of the eyes."

Among those watching Jaffe was seventy-eight-year-old Jerome Fisher, the founder of the Nine West shoe store chain, who reportedly lost $150 million to Madoff. Fisher was furious as he approached Jaffe. "What are you doing here?" he demanded. There was a shoving match as Fisher pushed Jaffe into the wall. "How could you?" he shouted as others moved in to separate the two men.

Trump was completely sympathetic to Fisher. "People went a little bit wild and you know what? They have every right to go wild because some of them lost a large percentage of their net worth. If he did that to me, if he got me to invest with Madoff, and Madoff turned out to be a total phony fraud, I wouldn't be very happy with Jaffe either."

The Bernie Madoff scandal rocked the genteel world of Palm Beach. Previous scandals involving then-Congressman Mark Foley and teenage boys, and the sensational divorce trial of the Pulitzers, were juicy tabloid fare. But this was serious. It involved real money. On the famed shopping street Worth Avenue, jewelry stores were doing big business buying up the gold and diamond jewelry of victims desperate to raise cash.

"I'm overwhelmed at the amount of jewelry from all these Madoff victims," said store owner Patti Esbia. "So much is coming in. I'm sure it had to be a sense of loss for them."

The Madoff scandal also served to shine a bright light on Palm Beach's infamous and ugly anti-Semitism.

Sitting around the kitchen table in her penthouse apartment, Ruth Madoff seethed about "the gentiles" who were gloating about her husband's downfall and its implication for the Jewish community.

"It's the fact that he's Jewish that is always associated with this," said Rabbi Michael Resnick at Temple Emanu-El of Palm Beach.

Town officials said they saw no sign of anti-Semitism in Palm Beach, before or after the Madoff arrest, but outside Rabbi Resnick's temple one Saturday morning, a member of the congregation who did not want to be named said non-Jewish friends had expressed "glee" about the plight of Madoff and his victims "as if we had it coming." "That's part of the great tragedy of this," said Rabbi Resnick, "because it reinforced the prejudice and the hatred that many people have toward Jews. This was a body blow to Judaism, and that's an equal tragedy in my mind." Jewish religious and community leaders in New York and Los Angeles expressed similar views, especially in light of the losses by Jewish charities that had invested their endowments with Madoff.

In an open letter to Madoff, published in *Newsweek,* Los Angeles rabbi Marc Gellman wrote, "You betrayed charities whose good works you have extinguished in an afternoon. These betrayals are epic in their scope and dazzling in their utter lack of remorse or responsibility. There must be some new word invented to describe the way you have redefined betrayal."

The records show that Madoff stole from Yeshiva University, Hadassah, the American Jewish Congress, Elie Wiesel's foundation, and a long list of other Jewish charities. By conservative estimates, charities lost almost $160 million.

There was little likelihood that the charities or any of Madoff's victims would recover anything approaching what they thought they had earned from their years of investment with Madoff. And in the efforts to recover Madoff's money, some of his customers came to feel they were being victimized twice.

Within days of the arrest, a federal bankruptcy judge put Madoff's firm into receivership and appointed a trustee, Irving Picard, to administer its affairs, locate any hidden money, and return as much to the victims as possible. Picard had already been chosen to handle the Madoff case for the Securities Investor Protection Corporation (SIPC), the government-backed agency that is supposed to make good on losses from brokerage and investment firms.

Investors are protected up to $500,000 by SIPC, with money that comes from all brokerage and investment firms in the country through a yearly assessment. Given the monumental size of the Madoff fraud, if every client got the maximum amount SIPC could be on the hook for more than $2 billion.

SIPC only had $1.6 billion in its reserve fund, and Picard soon made it clear that he would play hardball with the victims over how much they would receive. If everyone got the maximum, it would have required a short-term government loan and then a huge assessment on the country's broker-dealers to make up the shortfall.

Given the disarray of Madoff's records, it was difficult to figure out who was owed how much. The victims all had their monthly and quarterly statements, but those reflected what Picard called "false profits," the fictional amounts invented by Madoff. While the clients believed that's how much they had, Picard refused to recognize that number as his baseline. Instead, he decided he would completely discount any of the "false profits" and calculate the amount due victims based only on what each client had actually put into an account. And there was another catch. Picard said any amount that had been taken out of the account would be subtracted. This was a disaster for many of Madoff's longtime customers.

By Picard's math, if someone had invested a million dollars ten years ago and taken out a hundred thousand dollars each of those ten years, he would be due nothing. He had put a million in and taken a million out. Even if the fancy-looking monthly account statements indicated there was $2 million or $3 million in the account, the victim would be due nothing from SIPC. And if someone had taken out more than he put in over the years, Picard said he wanted the extra back. This was called a "clawback."

The victims were furious. Many had followed a prudent, conservative strategy of withdrawing just 10 percent each year as they watched their accounts grow, at least on paper. Many had used their withdrawals to pay income tax on the "false profits."

"Our clients were withdrawing money not to buy boats or go on vacation but to pay taxes on phony gains," said Brad Friedman of the Milberg law firm, who represents more than a hundred Madoff clients. "They got a statement that showed they had a gain and they had to pay taxes. They got 1099 IRS forms from Madoff. They took the money out to pay the government."

Picard's own lawyers calculated that the single biggest beneficiary of the Madoff scam was probably the IRS, because his victims had paid billions of dollars in tax on their "false profits."

"If Irv Picard wants to claw back money," said Friedman, "he should claw it back from the U.S. government." The IRS urged Madoff's victims to treat their losses as "theft deductions," which can be carried back up to five years or spread out over the next twenty years.

Some Madoff investors planned a different approach and intended to amend their previous tax returns so they could recoup what they paid in taxes on the "fake profits." But Congress has since changed the law to a three-year time limit for amending returns, making it even harder for Madoff's victims.

In June, 2015, many of the Madoff investors who had been subject to "clawbacks" got good news from the United States Supreme Court. The court let stand a lower court decision that Picard could not touch any of the money investors had withdrawn before December, 2006, or two years from the time the fraud was discovered. Picard calculated the decision would prevent him from collecting about $4.3 billion to distribute among those who were overall losers.

Despite what many thought, SIPC is not exactly the Wall Street version of the FDIC, which insures bank depositors. It does not consider itself to be offering insurance like the FDIC, which makes restitution up to $250,000 even in cases of bank fraud. Picard said the only "fair" way to treat everyone equally was on the "cash in, cash out" basis.

For example, one Madoff customer, Jeffry Picower, put in $1.7 billion but took out $6.7 billion. In other words, he took out $5 billion more in fictitious profits than he put into the twenty-four different Madoff accounts he controlled over a period of thirteen years, according to Picard's lawyers in a court filing. Picard's investigators discovered Picower's annual rates of return "were more than 100 percent, with some annual returns as high as 500 or even 950 percent per year."

Picower, a former attorney, accountant, and tax shelter promoter, was described by Picard as "a sophisticated investor" who was close to Madoff "on both a business and social level" for thirty years. In one account, Picard's lawyers found fifty-seven trades that "occurred" before the account was even opened. Picard believed Picower knew, or should have known, that Madoff's operation was a fraud, of which he was a principal beneficiary.

Picower's lawyer strongly denied the allegation.

For Picard, it was inconceivable that Picower should get a single penny from SIPC. In fact, he wanted the $5 billion that Picower had withdrawn returned so that it could be distributed to fellow investors who did not have the kind of relationship with Madoff that produced such "extraordinary and implausibly high rates of return."

"If we have to go to the government to get a loan and pay people like Picower and others who took out more than they put in, then, essentially, the American taxpayer is subsidizing all this," said one Picard lawyer.

Even so, there were a growing number of Madoff clients who were organizing "victims rights" and "victims coalition" groups to fight Picard's plan.

"People relied on those statements, they ordered their lives around those statements,; the purpose of the statute is to pay people based on those statements," said Milberg lawyer Brad Friedman. Picard "is trying to keep the payouts as low as possible so the brokerage industry doesn't have to reimburse the fund too much. He's acting like every insurance company that anyone has ever had difficulty with in just saying no. Figuring out ways not to pay the claim."

The government had a difficult time getting a "real number" about how big the Madoff scam had been. Madoff's first estimate to the FBI was $50 billion. Then a calculation of all the monthly client statements produced the number of more than $64 billion. But those were the inflated figures, based on the magic act that Bernie and others were cooking up on the seventeenth floor.

Investigators believe the "real number" will more likely be around $17.5 billion. That would still be the biggest Wall Street fraud ever.

There was plenty of anger to go around on the part of the victims, but few lost sight of the root cause of their trouble: Bernard L. Madoff.

William Foxton had had a distinguished career in the British army. He was decorated by the queen for his service around the time he retired and put his life savings of more than $3 million with Madoff.

Foxton's investment was made through one of Madoff's many salespeople, or fronts, the Bank Medici of Vienna, Austria. A chum told Foxton, "Get into this. It's great. It's totally safe."

Foxton was unaware that the high rates of return promised by the Austrian bank had anything to do with someone in New York of whom he had never heard before. An article in the British press said, "If you've got New York Jewish friends, then you're bound to know someone who has been hit by the scandal," recalled Foxton's son Willard. "And little did I know when I read the article that one person who had been affected by the scandal was actually me."

Slowly but surely, Willard's father became aware of the problem. "I'm having a huge fight with my bank," the senior Foxton wrote to his son in early February. "I think we might have lost everything. I think I might be bankrupt."

The money in the bank was all the family had. After years of service in Afghanistan and Oman, where he lost an arm in combat, the $3 million represented a dignified retirement, a quiet life the senior Foxton had earned after a career in the army. He was badly shaken.

On February 10, William Foxton took out his service revolver and put a bullet through his head. A second suicide had occurred that was tied to Madoff. Like the French banker, de la Villehuchet, Foxton had felt dishonored, his trust violated. He had let his family down.

"My father was an immensely proud man, and I think he would have hated the idea that he'd been gulled and fooled," said his son.

TEN

The Family

BERNIE MADOFF DISRUPTED AND DESTROYED MANY LIVES BUT none more than those of his own family. His sons, Andrew and Mark, never saw him again after the day he admitted his crimes to them and they went to the federal authorities.

On December 10, 2010, the second anniversary of that day, his eldest son, Mark, killed himself. His body was found hanging from a black dog leash in the living room of his Manhattan apartment. Mark's two-year-old son was asleep in a nearby bedroom.

Madoff's younger son, Andrew, died four years later after a battle with cancer. Their lives of privilege had collapsed and the burden of shame overtook them.

Thanks to their father, they were both multimillionaires. Madoff paid his boys big salaries at the family firm,
gave them Platinum American Express cards, loaned
them money for expensive homes, helped them through
divorces, and provided millions of dollars to their charitable foundations.

"We gave them everything," their mother, Ruth, would
later lament when Bernie's crimes split parents and children in an ugly family feud rife with accusations and
recriminations.

"Why don't you investigate those two boys?" said a
person close to Ruth Madoff. "You'll never find anyone
more self-serving."

"He was a crook and she was an enabler," said a person close to the sons, describing the boys' parents.

Andy was crushed by his father's arrest and the after-
math. "Now we're orphans," he told someone close to him.

The boys were raised amid wealth and privilege in the
New York suburb of Roslyn, on Long Island. There never
seemed to be any question that they would join the family
business.

"They started at the bottom," recalled Eleanor Squillari. "It was nice to see two brothers who were so close."
Although each had a distinctive personality. "Mark was
more vibrant and more noticeable. Andy's very reserved
and polite. He keeps to himself. He observes before he
gets to know you."

Even before they finished college, Bernie had the boys

come to the office. "When Mark first came in," Eleanor said, "Before he started working full-time, he used to sit out and answer the phones with me. He seemed to know so many of the people, because he grew up around these people."

According to federal prosecutors, their father's huge scam was secretly operating at full steam by the time his sons joined the firm.

Mark received a bachelor of arts in economics at the University of Michigan and joined the firm at age twenty-two, in 1986. Andy started working for his father in February 1988, at the age of twenty-two, after graduating from the University of Pennsylvania's Wharton School of Business with a bachelor of science in economics.

"He made them go to school, earn everything they got," said the former office messenger Little Rick, who remembers Mark and Andy at some of Bernie's wilder office parties. "Andy gave the persona of being uptight while Mark was more laid-back, liked the topless bars and stuff like that."

They could both be spoiled brats as young men. Little Rick says they infuriated their mother when they "trashed" a motel room in Montauk during one of the summer beach parties held for Madoff employees.

On another occasion, Little Rick says he had to intervene when Mark's close friend Jeff Wilpon had a heated argument with "one of our girls" at a Madoff firm Christmas party at a restaurant under the Brooklyn Bridge.

Wilpon is the son of one of Madoff's biggest investors, Fred Wilpon, the real estate developer, and now is a prominent public figure as the chief operating officer of the baseball team owned by his father, the New York Mets.

"Those kids grew up together, Jeff Wilpon and the Madoffs," said Little Rick. He said the younger Wilpon had arranged for his girlfriend, Linda, to work at the Madoff firm. And when she tried to break off their relationship, it turned ugly. Little Rick says that when the argument flared up inside the restaurant, he and another employee, known as "Big Rick," took Wilpon outside, "right by the edge of the river." The two Ricks, hired from the streets of Brooklyn and the Bronx, are not men to mess with. "And we told him, 'Listen, you're done. Don't ever do that again.'" A spokesman for Jeff Wilpon said Wilpon confirmed the relationship with Linda but did not recall the conversation with Big and Little Rick.

Mark and Andy's first assignment was the trading room of Madoff Securities. "I remember Mark said that he would prefer to answer the phones and his father was like, 'No, it's time for you to go in there.' It was a lot of pressure," explained Eleanor.

Bernie's boys soon took over the day-to-day management of the busy trading operation, sitting at a desk on an elevated platform, their father's office directly behind them. "He was able to look out and see his sons in the front," said Eleanor.

Everywhere he looked, a proud Bernie Madoff could

see family. Andy and Mark were at the trading desk. Ruth helped to keep the firm's books and balance the checking account from her office on the eighteenth floor. His younger brother, Peter, served as chief compliance officer and was the executive who oversaw Andy and Mark on the seventeenth floor. Peter's wife, Marion, was also on the company payroll, at $163,500 a year, although the bankruptcy trustee said there was no evidence that she did any work. Peter's daughter and Bernie's niece, Shana, became the firm's compliance lawyer after graduating from Fordham Law School in 1995. Peter's son, Roger, worked there briefly until his death from leukemia in 2006. Another Madoff nephew, Charlie Wiener, the son of Bernie and Peter's sister, Sondra, had started on the seventeenth floor in 1980.

"It was one big happy family," recalled a former employee. "They all seemed so clean-cut and close." Inside the family, however, there were some who feared Madoff, including his niece. "Shana tried to do everything perfect because she was afraid Bernie would yell at her," said Eleanor. All of the Madoffs, however, respected his power over them and regarded Bernie like the king of a royal family, or, some would say, the capo of a Mafia family. If the kingpin was taken out, all the other pins around him would be in jeopardy of falling, too.

Bernie, Ruth, Andy, and Mark worked together and went on vacation together. "In most families, people get up and go their own way and experience life on their own, but in this family they work together," recalled Eleanor. The sons could pull out their Platinum corporate American Express cards to pay for the grandest of family trips. The bill would go directly to the office and be paid by the family firm out of the account that held the funds for Madoff's investors. Every single member of the Madoff family connected to the business also had use of the corporate American Express cards, but the charges by the boys and Ruth were the most extravagant.

A January 2008 American Express bill shows that Andy and Mark used their cards to pay for a family ski vacation in Jackson Hole, Wyoming, over the Christmas and New Year's holiday. There are thousands of dollars in charges for restaurants, clothing, ski tickets, ski lessons, groceries, and rental cars. Bernie and Ruth flew in on one of their private jets to join the family at the Teton Village resort just outside Jackson Hole. Lots of snow, kids on skis, family dinners at the Mangy Moose at the base of the ski lifts—a wonderful time, all expenses paid by the company. What a great grandfather.

The credit card records now in the hands of the FBI and the bankruptcy trustee show a pattern of vacations and other personal expenditures that, because they were paid for by the company, the IRS would consider taxable income that must be declared by the recipient. Failure to report income is a federal crime.

Although Mark and Andy's rise to the top was not unexpected, former employees say they proved their mettle to

their father in the fast-paced trading on the nineteenth
floor. "Here's a guy who pushed his kids to learn everything about the stock market that they could," said Little
Rick. "He was very big on them succeeding." Andy would
later pull back from the business after his diagnosis and
treatment for lymphoma. He was still employed at his
father's firm but spent more time away from the office
and actually took over a business that produced reels for
fly-fishing.

Andy and Mark did not work on the seventeenth floor,
where the criminal scheme was being run, but Madoff
apparently told one of his biggest investors that his
sons gave him trading advice for that part of the business. In testimony before the Securities and Exchange
Commission in 2007, Jeff Tucker, the cofounder of Fairfield Greenwich, was asked if he knew any of the people
besides Madoff and Frank DiPascali who were involved in
making investment decisions.

"Going back some time," testified Tucker, "Bernie
once or twice said, 'You know, I may consult with my kids,
who run the trading room, because they get a good feel
for where the market is.'"

"So the two kids, was it Andrew Madoff was one of
them and—?" asked the SEC lawyer.

"Andrew and Mark," replied Tucker.

Madoff's statement to Tucker was a lie on at least one
level. He never made any trades for his investors, so there

would be no reason he would consult with his sons about which trades to make. Nevertheless, by invoking Andy and Mark's names, Madoff was able to pull the wool over Tucker's eyes. At another point, Madoff also told Fairfield Greenwich that if he were to die suddenly, his sons or brother would take over the investment advisory business. If nothing else, he used his sons to carry on the deceit, because planting the idea of them by his side picking stocks or ready to succeed him helped bolster his image.

The sons told the FBI they were completely unaware of their father's crimes until he confessed to them on December 10.

Others on Wall Street have said that if Mark and Andy did not know, they should have known. Given Madoff's sons' day-to-day involvement in the market, many wondered how they could not have noticed their father's lack of trades and realized that something was wrong. Madoff did not like titles, but his son Mark was considered the head of trading.

"That the sons didn't question the fact that there was no volume in the securities that they were making markets in, which Madoff was supposedly trading," said Suzanne Murphy, a hedge fund adviser, raised lots of questions. "'Dad, hey, why aren't we doing these trades?' They had to know something funny was going on, because they weren't doing the trades."

According to the bankruptcy trustee, both Mark and

Andy had accounts with their father. "So, presumably, they were getting statements," said Murphy. "And if they had looked at their statements, they would've said, 'Wait a second.'"

Madoff's cover story for the lack of trades in the New York office was that all of the trades were being handled through the European markets by the London office, Madoff Securities International, Ltd. His employees in London have since told British and American investigators that, other than a small volume for Madoff's personal accounts, they never made any such trades. Both Mark and Andy had been directors of the London business since 1998, and in that role they had the ability, and some would say the fiduciary responsibility, to learn the truth.

Like many others, however, the two sons had plenty of reasons not to push their father on the way he did business. He always took care of them.

Madoff gave Mark a $5 million loan while he was married to his first wife, Susan, with whom he had two children, Daniel and Katherine. According to records filed in his divorce proceedings in 1999, Mark was then making $770,000 a year working for his father. His "periodic dividends" from his partial ownership of the London office were applied to pay the interest on the $5 million loan from his father.

In June, 2008, Mark again used his father's money to buy a $6.5 million beach house on Nantucket, the exclusive island retreat off Cape Cod. The home is on the ocean in the Tom Nevers section, with five bedrooms, four baths, a hot tub, and separate guest quarters. The money came directly from the firm's accounts as a "loan" to Mark and his second wife, Stephanie, at 3.2 percent a year. An investigator for the bankruptcy trustee found no "records of any interest or principal" being repaid by Mark and "no apparent benefit" to the firm for offering the loan. In effect, money stolen by his father paid for Mark's summer beach house.

Although he was the younger brother, Andy was no less well rewarded for being Bernie's son. The foundation he set up with his then-estranged wife, the Deborah and Andrew Madoff Foundation, had more than $4 million. Andy had survived a scare with lymphoma in 2003, and his parents "doted on their baby," according to someone close to Ruth.

Even as the markets neared collapse in September of 2008 and Madoff was beginning to see trouble on the horizon, he still had enough money to help Andy buy a $4 million apartment in New York City, on East Seventy-fourth Street, overlooking the East River. Andrew closed on the property October 6, three weeks after the bankruptcy of Lehman Brothers, when his father was already in a desperate scramble to raise money from new and old victims and avoid the detection of his crimes. The $4 million came directly from the money investors entrusted to Madoff.

Mark's home in Nantucket and Andy's New York

apartment were financed by Madoff at a time the government contends his criminal scheme was well under way. His decision to "confess" to his two sons and arrange for them to call the FBI was designed to divert any suspicion of Andy and Mark. But for many, it seemed too obvious.

"What would you do if you were a father trying to protect his sons?" asked Suzanne Murphy. "'I'm going to say you knew nothing about it, because I'm seventy years old, you're forty, you've got children. So I will take the fall for this.' It's probably the only menschy Jewish thing he's done."

If nothing else, Mark and Andy faced the almost certain loss of anything they owned that was paid for by their father. The boys refused to see their father in prison or to speak to their mother. All their communications were through lawyers. Bernie wrote to his grandchildren, but Mark would not allow his children from his first or second marriages to visit their grandfather in prison or their grandmother in her apartment. They had exchanged letters with their grandfather in prison, but they wanted to change their last name to avoid the shame associated with anything Madoff.

Ruth was livid with both of her sons. She found their behavior "unconscionable" and "outrageous." She told someone close to her that she understood how her sons feel but that their behavior toward her was "unforgivable." She ranted that they didn't understand what she was going through. They had their families and the outside world. She only had them. Mark and his wife, Stephanie, sent Ruth a birth announcement for the newest Madoff, Nicholas Henry, but there was no invitation for Grandma to visit. Ruth told others in the family that only Mark's ex-wife, Susan, seemed to have the decency to send her support.

Other members of the Madoff family had their own problems to worry about as they faced the likelihood of financial ruin and the possibility of criminal prosecution.

As the chief compliance officer, Madoff's brother, Peter, had attested to the firm's legitimacy to the SEC for years. But his significant role in the business did not mean that he enjoyed the best of relationships with his older brother. The firm was in Bernie's name; it was not Madoff Brothers Securities, and Bernie had never considered making his younger brother his full partner.

Family friends say Bernie could be cruel to Peter at times. Bernie and Peter and their families did not vacation together or even spend major Jewish holidays together. After the death of his son, Roger, in 2006, Peter became very religious and would go to the Park Avenue Synagogue every morning before heading to the office. According to a family friend, Peter's wife kept a kosher kitchen, while Bernie used to boast in Peter's presence that his own favorite food was "pork sausage."

Even so, Peter's role in filling out the SEC documents and forms—regardless of whether he knew about the Ponzi scheme under way on the seventeenth floor—left him in the sights of the FBI and the SEC, as well as the teams of lawyers circling on behalf of cheated customers. "His brother was either involved or is going to have to proffer a defense that he was the stupidest man in America," said Brad Friedman of the Milberg firm, which represents Madoff victims.

In a 2012 plea agreement, Peter Madoff pleaded guilty to one count of conspiracy to commit securities fraud and one count of falsifying records. He was sentenced to ten years in prison.

Peter was a major beneficiary of his brother's largesse. In December 2007, Bernie loaned him $9 million around the time Peter bought his daughter an expensive weekend home in the Hamptons. The loan was repayable to Bernie personally, even though the money came from the same account at JPMorgan Chase where investors' funds were deposited. The bankruptcy trustee found no "records of any interest or principal ever being paid" to the firm on this loan.

In 2008, Bernie used money from the investors' account to buy Peter a $237,600 rare 1964 vintage Aston Martin. He had it delivered to Peter's home in Palm Beach. "That was his baby," recalled Eleanor Squillari. "He was in a terrible place after the death of his son, and this was helping him get out of it." The car was later seized by trustees handling the bankruptcy of Madoff's London office.

But Peter had much more to worry about than the loss

of his gem of a sports car. His wife, Marion, and daughter, Shana, both had their own issues with the Madoff family business. The three of them each had one of the firm's Corporate Platinum American Express cards, which they used for a variety of what appear to be personal charges. Peter used the card to fly his wife and himself to Tel Aviv and Milan in September 2008. Marion charged expensive meals at New York restaurants. Shana and her husband used the card to fly to Cancún, Mexico. Potentially more troubling was Marion's no-show job at the Madoff firm. The yearly payment to her of $163,500 for no apparent work was seen by some investigators as part of a family conspiracy to defraud investors.

And of even more concern was the role Shana played as the firm's compliance lawyer. She dealt directly with the SEC in filing a variety of regulatory statements required of financial firms. Investigators say large numbers of the SEC compliance documents filed by the Madoff firm over the years "contain outright misstatements of facts."

Although Shana's responsibilities as a compliance lawyer mainly involved the legitimate trading operation on the nineteenth floor, she was also involved in preparing Bernie's 2007 investment adviser licensing application to the SEC, according to investigators and people with knowledge of the situation. The application was full of lies, and one of the counts Madoff pleaded guilty to involved the false statements on the form.

Asked on the application to provide the number of clients to whom Madoff provided investment advisory services, someone checked the box "eleven to twenty-five." A truthful answer would have been more than 4,900.

Madoff signed the form, but even if his niece only included information she was told by others, it put her in the eyes of the bankruptcy trustee. She never faced criminal charges, but forfeited her assets to settle the trustee's civil claims against her.

Michael Wolk, a lawyer for Shana and her husband, Eric Swanson, said, "It would be inappropriate for us to comment beyond reiterating that Ms. Swanson had no knowledge of Mr. Madoff's wrongdoing." Shana told people that the first she knew about the scam was when her father told her Uncle Bernie had just been arrested on December 11.

Other than Bernie, of course, no one named Madoff received more attention and investigative scrutiny than Ruth. The bankruptcy trustee charged that she had lived a "life of splendor" with money "she knew, or should have known" belonged to her husband's business and investigators. The bank accounts scrutinized after Madoff's arrest showed that in the last six years alone more than $44 million was transferred from the business directly into her accounts or to pay for her investments in other companies. "The Madoff Ponzi scheme massively enriched" Mrs. Madoff, the bankruptcy trustee charged, and filed court papers to recapture that amount. It was an effort to "make sure she had nothing left," according to one investigator.

There continued to be great suspicion of how she could possibly "not have known" of her husband's crime spree. She was by Bernie's side from the very beginning when she kept the firm's books.

People close to her say she was simply reconciling deposits and payments, without knowing the underlying scheme that was at the heart of the business that provided her with such a fine lifestyle.

Perhaps it was an exaggeration, but Ruth had boasted to old high school friends of her role in setting up the family business in the 1960s, and Bernie also spoke of Ruth's business acumen. At an industry seminar, Madoff described the evolution of the firm's computerized trading operation and Ruth's help in making decisions on staff. "Actually it was my wife who said, 'Why don't you hire math people? Why don't you go to MIT and hire math people, because everything you're doing is related to algorithmic trading and they're probably the best people,'" Madoff said. Based on that description, Ruth seemed to at least have a firm grasp on her husband's legitimate trading business.

Ruth also had a Corporate Platinum American Express card, which she used freely for her personal benefit. Investigators for the bankruptcy trustee found that she had charged more than $3.2 million for personal expenses since 2002.

She charged dinners, museum memberships, boat-docking fees, and charitable contributions. Lavish parties, private jet travel, expensive antiques, and an unlimited budget for clothing were all things she had become accustomed to. As long as Bernie's decades-long crime spree had endured, her life had been one without any worry about money.

Beyond her role in keeping the books, investigators focused on Ruth's actions in the months before her husband's arrest. From accounts connected to her husband's firm, she twice made withdrawals, which together totaled $15.5 million. The last withdrawal, for $10 million, occurred on the morning Bernie set in motion his arrest with the "confession" to his sons.

"I don't think it's unreasonable to surmise that it had to do with Madoff's expected surrender," said secretary of the commonwealth William Galvin, whose investigators were the first to discover Ruth's withdrawals and informed the FBI and SEC. "I think it raised sufficient questions for me that we referred this matter" to the FBI and the SEC, he said. A belief publicly unspoken by the investigators is that Ruth's actions were an illegal effort to get money out and hide it before the firm collapsed.

Even if she had been unaware of her husband's Ponzi scheme over the years, investigators say the timing of the withdrawals and transfers raised a number of suspicions.

"Whatever motivated her to claim these funds at the time she did," said Galvin, her choice to do so "certainly makes it questionable as to what her motive was or what she might have known."

Whatever she had in mind, federal prosecutors determined she had not broken the law.

ELEVEN

Guilty

ON MARCH 12, 2009, MADOFF PLEADED GUILTY TO ELEVEN counts of fraud, money laundering, and perjury before U.S. District Court judge Denny Chin.

"For many years up until my arrest on December 11, 2008, I operated a Ponzi scheme," began Madoff in front of the crowded New York courtroom. The room was full of journalists, federal agents, and his victims. Every seat was taken. There was another room on the first floor with a video feed playing on two large screens for the overflow crowd.

Outside, dozens of cameras and satellite trucks were at full power. Madoff's trip downtown from his penthouse apartment in the security company's black SUV had been tracked by television station helicopters. Bernie Madoff was finally facing justice, with the sort of attention reserved for only the most celebrated American criminals.

From the beginning, there had been so much anger from Madoff's cheated clients that his private security detail ordered him to wear a bulletproof vest when he left the apartment for his many court appearances.

"It wasn't going to be the old couple that was going to come after Madoff, it was going to be the potential heir, the son of a victim who would come after him," said Nick Casale, a former New York City police detective whose private investigative firm was hired to make sure Madoff met the terms of his court-approved house arrest and to make sure no one killed him before he went to court.

"You have people who are looking to make a name for themselves, and you have your normal emotionally disturbed person walking the streets of New York City," explained Casale. "And there was some scuttlebutt about potential threats from South America and eastern Europe."

Madoff asked Casale, "Do you really think I need this?"

"Yes," said Casale, helping the seventy-year-old man put on his vest. He saw no emotion in Madoff's face.

Casale had spent hours in the Madoff penthouse apartment between the time Madoff was arrested and when he finally was sent to jail after pleading guilty. He gained a rare look inside the life that Bernie Madoff had lived after his arrest.

"He was somebody who had stepped back from his inner soul," said Casale. "He was almost blank." Before one court session, when it seemed entirely possible that the judge would order Madoff jailed instead of allowing him to head back to Ruth, he appeared completely indifferent.

"Do you want a moment to say good-bye to Ruth, a moment to be alone?" Casale asked him.

"No," said Madoff, and then, Casale said, he "put on his coat, his jacket, and we left." There were no good-bye hugs with Ruth, no tears, no emotion.

When the judge allowed him to go home that day, there was, similarly, no joy, no emotion. "The same face riding into court as returning back home," said Casale, who said he had seen the same lack of emotion in serial killers.

"Not somebody who would commit a crime out of opportunity or passion." It had all been carefully planned.

Even though he was in disgrace and faced spending the rest of his life in prison, Madoff did not appear to his guards to be a suicide risk, and there was no effort to seal off the kitchen terrace on the twelfth floor of his luxury building on East Sixty-fourth Street.

"I don't believe that ever crossed his mind," said Casale.

At one point, his sons Mark and Andy received an e-mail from their father that they thought sounded a lot like a suicide note. "Please take care of your mother after I am gone," read the note, according to someone familiar with the event. Mark and Andy were not moved. They called their lawyers, who notified prosecutors that Bernie might be about to end it all. Madoff was amused at the fuss. He had just been preparing for his life in prison, he said. He had no plans and no reason to take his life.

"Antisocial personalities, because they are so narcissistic and self-centered, rarely kill themselves," said former FBI agent and criminal profiler Brad Garrett. "It's like 'There's nothing wrong with me, you're the one that has a problem. The rest of the world has a problem, but not me.'"

In fact, Madoff's security detail was more concerned about Ruth's demeanor than Bernie's. People around her after her husband's arrest say she was stunned and not taking the news very well. She appeared to some to be drugged or drunk and extremely despondent. Antidepressant pills became part of her daily diet.

Ruth would later claim that she and Bernie both tried, unsuccessfully, to commit suicide by taking an overdose of sleeping pills one evening.

Life in the penthouse apartment during those three months between the December arrest and the March guilty plea was surprisingly banal, according to Casale, who was in and out of the apartment as part of his security duties. While he was there, he saw firsthand Madoff's anal-retentive side. "Here I am with the fraudster of the century," said Casale, "and he was acting like a house-keeper. He wanted to make sure everything was in place, prim and proper."

When Casale's men nicked the paint on the molding in his expansive closet, Madoff brought out the vacuum cleaner himself and tidied up. "Look, we'll have some-body come up, one of the handymen, and just touch it up," offered Casale.

"No," said Madoff, "I'll take care of it."

"It had to be his way, and, you know, he can do it bet-ter than they could," recalled Casale. "People like that, who micromanage, it's the minutiae, the little things in life that upset them. With the weight of the world on his shoulders, a little thing like that meant something to him."

Otherwise, Casale said, Madoff seemed to accept his plight. Besides the fact that he wasn't going to the office every day, Bernie and Ruth kept up a fairly normal rou-tine as they perused the morning papers and talked about everything but the Ponzi scheme.

Downstairs, photographers and protestors were a daily presence. "We had people standing outside screaming at the apartment, carrying posters," said Casale.

The Madoffs were barely moved. "They were united with each other," said Casale. "They were together. It was almost like nothing outside the apartment was occurring.

There was strength between the two of them, and there was love and compassion."

Madoff asked Casale what to expect in prison. Casale described a harsh life, but Madoff seemed "indifferent." He wasn't even bothered that he would soon only have one orange jumpsuit to his name. "It'll be like the time I spent at the Army Reserves at Fort Bragg," he told his wife.

For the long-anticipated day of his guilty plea, Madoff wore his bulletproof vest over his usual dark suit, white shirt, and a black woven-knit tie. He might be going to prison, but he would do so looking like a French diplomat. Ruth did not accompany him to court, telling friends she was unable to bear the sight and that she feared being confronted by one of her husband's victims.

"All rise," said the bailiff as Judge Chin took the bench. "Mr. Sorkin, your client is still prepared to plead guilty today as we discussed on Thursday?" the judge asked Madoff's lawyer, Ike Sorkin. "Yes, Your Honor."

As Madoff stood, the judge asked him, "Mr. Madoff, do you understand that you are now under oath and that if you answer my questions falsely, your untrue answers may later be used against you in another prosecution for perjury or making false statements?"

"Yes, I do," said Madoff, who, according to federal prosecutors, would proceed to lie to the judge. He had already been informed that federal sentencing guidelines called for him to serve 150 years, and the prospect of prosecution for perjury was an empty threat.

Madoff's voice was dry, and the judge asked for some water for him.

The federal prosecutor, Marc Litt, read the indictment into the record. Having been conned earlier by Madoff's false promise of full cooperation, Litt was eager to assert control. Madoff was not going to win this round.

"Mr. Madoff," said the judge, "would you tell me what you did, please?"

"Your Honor," began Madoff, reading word-for-word from the written statement crafted by his lawyers, "I am actually grateful for this first public opportunity to speak about my crimes, for which I am so deeply sorry and ashamed.

"As I engaged in my fraud, I knew what I was doing was wrong, indeed criminal," he continued. "When I began the Ponzi scheme, I believed it would end shortly and I would be able to extricate myself and my clients from the scheme. However, this proved difficult, and ulti-mately impossible, and as the years went by I realized that my arrest and this day would inevitably come."

Few of the many FBI agents, prosecutors, and inves-tigators on the case believed a word Madoff said that day, "other than the word guilty," claimed one investigator.

"I am painfully aware that I have deeply hurt many, many people," Madoff continued, in a monotone voice, without apparent emotion, "including the members of my family, my closest friends, business associates, and the thousands of clients who gave me their money."

"That's what you're supposed to say," said former FBI agent Garrett. "You can't walk in and say, 'You know, I had a great time screwing these people and I'd really love to do it again,' which is really probably what he's thinking in his own mind, but you have to tell the court what you think they want to hear. What's fascinating is that there really is no remorse. He said he hurt people, but it's basically all about him."

Madoff described his version of how the scheme worked, without referring to any family member or employee who might have helped him. He made a particular point in his statement of defending the part of the firm run by his brother and two sons as "legitimate, profitable, and successful in all respects." Investigators say that, at the very least, money from the two sides of the business was commingled. Madoff was also well aware that he had made his brother and sons directors of the London office, which he used as a front for the illegal activity.

Madoff also made no mention of how he had used the hundreds of millions of dollars he had stolen to pay for the life of wealth and privilege he provided to Ruth, his brother, his sons, other family members, and employees who were part of his inner circle.

Then came a crucial detail. When did the scam begin?

"To the best of my recollection, my fraud began in the early 1990s," said Madoff under oath. This was a statement that the government immediately contradicted when he was through.

"The government does not entirely agree with all of the defendant's description of his conduct," said prosecutor Litt. If there had been a trial, the government said it could have proved "the defendant operated a massive Ponzi scheme though his company, Bernard L. Madoff Investment Securities, beginning at least as early as the 1980s."

Much rides on the determination of the start date of Madoff's Ponzi scheme. By maintaining that it began in the early 1990s, Madoff and his lawyers are able to argue that properties bought prior to that date, including the New York apartment and the Montauk beach house, were bought with legitimately earned money.

Perhaps most astounding to the victims who had been invited to court to listen to Madoff's guilty plea was his explanation for why he did it.

"While I never promised a specific rate of return to any client, I felt compelled to satisfy my clients' expectations, at any cost," Madoff said.

In Madoff's version, it wasn't his greed that led to a life of crime, but the greed of his clients. If only they hadn't been so demanding. If only they hadn't believed the recruiters and feeder funds who raised billions for Madoff by promising rates of return that Madoff was now trying to deny he had ever encouraged anyone to believe.

At heart, Madoff had about as much sympathy for

the rest of his clients as he did for the French aristocrat banker who committed suicide. It was their fault, not his.

"That is a key component of antisocial personalities," said former FBI agent Garrett. "'I made those people a bunch of money, and they're idiots anyway. They would have made crappy investments without me, me, the Big Bernie.'"

Several of his victims were in court and tried to approach him. One of them, George Nierenberg, demanded that Madoff look him in the eye. "He turned around and looked at me, but he didn't look at the other victims," said Nierenberg.

Another victim, Ronnie Sue Ambrosino, asked the judge to reject the plea. "I believe that you have the opportunity today to find out information as to where the money is and to find out who else may be involved in this crime. And if the plea is accepted without those two pieces of information, then I do object."

Some of the agents and investigators in the courtroom quietly agreed. Madoff had refused to cooperate in government efforts to reconstruct his crime and track the money he was suspected of hiding overseas. Investigators believe there could be a billion dollars or more that Madoff, always the careful planner, had stashed in foreign bank accounts. If so, he did a good job hiding it because no such funds have been located.

A third victim, Maureen Ebel, said a full criminal trial

would show the world "that all crimes, all crimes, including crimes of greed, can be dissected, ruled upon, and punished."

Judge Chin said the guilty plea accomplished the same purpose. He accepted Madoff's plea and revoked his bail.

"Mr. Madoff has pled guilty; he is no longer entitled to the presumption of innocence. The exposure is great, 150 years in prison. In light of Mr. Madoff's age, he has an incentive to flee, he has the means to flee, and thus he presents a risk of flight," ruled the judge.

U.S. marshals moved forward to take Madoff to jail. Outside the courtroom he was put in handcuffs and walked through an underground tunnel that led from the federal courthouse to the Metropolitan Correctional Center, a federal prison that has housed some of the country's most notorious criminals. Madoff was sent to cellblock SHU, the special housing unit. Several other accused white-collar criminals were in the same section of the jail, but he was the king of them all.

Ike Sorkin called Ruth to tell her that Bernie would not be coming home this time. Or anytime soon. Ruth had known the odds were against him remaining free any longer, but Ike's call was devastating. Her only comfort, she told family members, was that she was relieved to hear from Bernie's lawyers that the prison "wasn't as brutal" as she and Bernie had been initially warned it would be.

Now Ruth, too, became a prisoner. She was afraid to leave her apartment because of all the reporters and her fear that she would run into one of her husband's angry clients on the streets of Manhattan. Ruth used her security guards, who were still being paid out of the investors' funds, to do her errands. She even found a way to sneak out of her apartment building by using a door in the building that connected to the back of a stationery store that opened onto Lexington Avenue, around the corner from her building's main entrance, where the camera crews were camped.

She told people close to her she felt lonely and shunned. She withdrew from the country clubs on Long Island and in Palm Beach where she and Bernie played golf. She was afraid they wouldn't let her have her golf bag and clubs back, but they did. But her social shunning was widespread.

Pierre Michel, her hair salon for the last ten years, told her she was no longer welcome. To add to the humiliation, the owners actually issued a public statement after the story broke on Page Six, the *New York Post*'s gossip page. "The Pierre Michel salon's clients are among some of the Manhattan's most elite," the statement read. "Unfortunately some of those clients were victims of the Madoff's [sic] and therefore Pierre Michel didn't feel comfortable having her in the salon." Not only had the self-described "magnet for celebrities, socialites, fashionists and trendsetters" banned Ruth, but they ascribed some of the blame for the scam to her. "Victims of the Madoff's [sic]," their statement read, not "victims of her husband." At $125 and up for a haircut, and $200 and up for highlights, Ruth probably would have had to find a new place to tend to her blond bob, anyway. But the sting of rejection was still sharp.

Within days of the guilty plea, Ruth began to witness the dismemberment of the empire of wealth she and Bernie had built. She told one family member it was a relief to have one less possession when she learned the $7 million yacht, *The Bull*, was being sold in France.

But when the federal government made plans to sell the Manhattan penthouse and seized the Palm Beach waterfront estate and the home in Montauk, Ruth told family friends it was heartbreaking to lose all the beautiful things they had accumulated over the years.

Ruth worried that the government wouldn't know what to do with their fine antiques, and might not sell them for as much as they could in order to pay back the investors. She was especially upset when she saw the list of items being sold along with the Madoff villa on the Riviera. The oil painting she and Bernie bought in New York for $35,000 was being sold for 500 euros. The furniture they bought at antique fairs in London and Paris was not being treated as it should be. It wasn't simply used furniture; these were antiques, Ruth reportedly fumed. The woman whose husband had stolen the money to buy her precious objects said she hated to see the new buyers practically steal the stuff at such a good price from the bumbling government.

Bernie Madoff spent his seventy-first birthday in jail on April 29. Ruth visited him a few days earlier on her normal Monday visiting schedule, but there was no cake and no trip to Cabo San Lucas like the previous year. Prison officials say "there are no birthday celebrations permitted in federal prison."

Also, according to federal prison rules, hugging, embracing, and kissing are allowed but not conjugal visits.

Ruth continued to profess her love for Bernie, but she began to plan her life without him. She told family members that she had begun to clean the penthouse on her own. The cleaning ladies for the Madoffs' homes in New York and Palm Beach, who had all been paid from company accounts, were let go. Ruth cried when her New York maid, Praxides Dirilo, left, but she felt better after she went out and bought a Swiffer to do her own cleaning. Ruth told friends she had begun to "feel free," apparently exulting now in the lifting of the burden of so many expensive possessions that had defined her life as Madoff's wife.

As the news coverage of her husband's scandal died down a bit, there were sometimes days when no stories about them appeared in either the *Wall Street Journal* or the *New York Times*. Those were good days for Ruth, who began to hope that maybe there would be an end to all the attention. She was thinking of going back to her gym, hoping she would be welcome.

For several years, Ruth remained estranged from her

sons, Andy and Mark, who considered her an enabler of their father. At their lawyer's insistence, she was told to communicate with the boys only through the lawyers. The grandchildren were not included in the lawyer's dictum, and Ruth cherished the thought of spending time with them and reading their messages. She even understood why they wanted to change their name to anything but Madoff.

She knew the world was angry at Bernie and at her. Ruth's own sister, Joan, and Joan's daughter, Diane, had lost everything they invested with Bernie, but they continued to see Ruth. Ruth confided to a friend that, in what must have been a strange scene, she had even traveled to Long Island to help out with a yard sale Diane had been forced to hold because of Bernie's crimes. She said she felt miserable the whole time, knowing her husband and his scheme had ruined the life of her favorite niece.

While Ruth suffered for her husband's crimes, Bernie seemed to be a new man in prison. He was immune to the cameras outside and the daily drumbeat of investigative reports. Ruth told one person that Bernie sounded free and no longer burdened by the necessity of keeping a multibillion-dollar Ponzi scheme going. He no longer had to check the daily bank balances or make sure the SEC wasn't closing in. According to someone familiar with his daily life inside, Bernie passed the time reading John Grisham novels.

Only one more event was left in his rapid descent from

multimillionaire to imprisoned felon. Judge Chin would sentence him for his crimes, and the outcome could have a significant impact on his day-to-day life and comfort.

There had been no deal struck between Bernie's lawyers and federal prosecutors when he agreed to plead guilty to the eleven felony counts. He had refused to offer the FBI any further cooperation in unraveling his finances or incriminating others. Madoff expected to spend the rest of his life in prison. He knew he would likely die behind bars. The actual length of the sentence, however, would determine the kind of federal prison where he would be sent.

A sentence in the twenty-year range could mean he would be eligible for a medium security prison, where the restrictions on inmate life allow a more relaxed daily existence and his fellow inmates would be a less hardened lot. If he were given the maximum sentence of 150 years, he faced the possibility of being sent to a maximum security prison, where his worst nightmares might be realized. He feared being attacked. Violent gangs often control significant portions of such facilities. Inmates are forced to take sides to find protectors in order to survive. Would Bernie's skill at manipulation and deceit work as well in prison as it had in the Lipstick Building?

Some thought Madoff had little to worry about. "The prisons are full of antisocial personalities who thrive there," said former FBI agent Garrett. "He can be the king of the court again but in a jail environment. If every day it's all about you and doing whatever you want to do, you're not going to be depressed. You're not going to be anything. You're going to try to find somebody else to manipulate and control."

Madoff had made his fortune through manipulation. Other celebrity inmates had found ways to use their infamy to get cushy work details and gain respect from their new neighbors. After all, who had ever stolen more or better shown up the "feds" as incompetent bumblers? "He can create an environment that he controls in prison, so people look up to him and he's holding forth and they're coming to his cell and asking questions. That would be predictable."

Still, Madoff was worried about being sent to a maximum security facility, and he began to craft a new statement to read at his sentencing hearing that would actually offer an apology to his victims. The master con man knew what to do.

TWELVE

Life

A HUSH FELL OVER THE CROWDED COURTROOM AS BERNARD Madoff was brought in to face sentencing on June 29, 2009.

The now seventy-one-year-old con man seemed thinner than he'd been when he'd appeared three months earlier to enter his guilty plea. Life in his temporary prison home, the federal Metropolitan Correctional Center in Lower Manhattan, had been more of a strain than he'd expected. His grayish white hair had thinned in the front, but it had grown much longer in the back, curled up like some aging European playboy's.

He wore the same dark suit, white shirt, and black tie

that he had worn in March, but now he looked disheveled. The suit was wrinkled, and worse, for a man who once obsessed about his clothing and appearance, the collars of his shirt turned up like unruly flaps. Madoff tried to press them down, but to no avail. After his last court appearance, his suit had been swapped by prison guards for a blue jumpsuit and held in reserve for this final court appearance. If his collar stays had been sterling silver or brass, as they likely would have been for a gentleman of means such as Madoff, they would have been confiscated because prison rules prohibit any metal objects. The Bureau of Prisons does not provide plastic collar stays. Bernie Madoff looked a mess.

"Crook," shouted one of his former investors seated in the front row of the courtroom as Madoff took his seat. Hundreds of onetime clients had lined up outside the courthouse for the opportunity to see the day of reckoning for the man who had betrayed and robbed them.

"This is the end of Bernie Madoff," said one of his victims, Michael DeVita, as he waited to get through the large crowd drawn to the spectacle. Network and local television programs were doing live shots from across the street. Many of the victims had their own public relations representatives to schedule interviews. Someone was selling copies of comedian Andy Borowitz's book *Who Moved My Soap?: The CEO's Guide to Surviving Prison: The Bernie Madoff Edition*. Bars of soap inscribed with Madoff's face and attached to a rope were being handed out to passersby. With the addition of a guillotine, it could have been a scene from Charles Dickens's *A Tale of Two Cities*. "You jerk," said the daughter of one victim, Jen Morrow, when reporters asked her what she would like to say to Madoff. "How could you possibly do this? I hope that your family never lives a life of luxury."

Madoff said nothing as he was escorted by U.S. marshals to the defense table, where he was seated with his lead lawyer, Ike Sorkin, on his left. As Sorkin conferred with his partner, Dan Horwitz, Madoff took two folded pieces of paper from his suit jacket. They contained the handwritten statement he would read to the judge in a last effort to appear contrite and again seek to exonerate his wife, sons, and brother.

Judge Denny Chin had moved the hearing to the large ceremonial courtroom on the ninth floor of the federal courthouse in Lower Manhattan so there would be more room for the many victims and journalists who wanted to attend. The reporters took up the right side of the room and the victims were on the left. The first two rows were reserved for nine victims who had asked to speak. In the jury box, six sketch artists drew the scene to provide a visual record for television and newspaper coverage.

At the prosecution table, across from Madoff, assistant United States attorneys Lisa Baroni, Marc Litt, and Barbara Ward were joined by an assortment of federal agents who had worked on the case. Baroni had replaced Litt as the lead government lawyer, apparently in response to criticism that Litt had initially been too easy on Madoff. Indeed, Litt himself told associates that Madoff had conned him into thinking he would cooperate if he was permitted to stay out of jail under house arrest at his penthouse apartment. Once Litt agreed to the house arrest, Madoff then refused to cooperate. Officials at the Department of Justice in Washington were determined not to let Madoff pull another fast one.

Conspicuous by her absence this morning was Ruth Madoff, who continued to pay the price for her husband's crimes. A few days earlier she had given up her fight to keep the New York penthouse. The government had already seized the Madoffs' vacation homes in Montauk, Palm Beach, and France. Ruth's lawyer's effort to prove she and Bernie had, at least, bought the $7 million apartment with legitimate money had failed. In an agreement with prosecutors, Ruth would be allowed to keep just $2.5 million of the hundreds of millions the family once had. She was no bag lady, but with no place to live, she had become homeless. Ruth was afraid of what would happen if she showed her face at the courthouse, and so she stayed home.

In fact, no member of Madoff's family was present to lend him support. No one even had the time or interest to send a letter. "I would expect to see letters from family and friends and colleagues," said Judge Chin. "But not a single letter has been submitted attesting to Mr. Madoff's good deeds or good character or civic or charitable activities. The absence of such support is telling."

There was no shortage of condemnation, however, as the victims stepped to a microphone to tell their stories of economic ruin and emotional devastation. Madoff was seated in front of them and they could only see his back and the curls of his hair.

Tears rolled down the cheeks of Don Ambrosino, a retired New York City corrections officer, whose life savings were wiped out in the Madoff scam. His dream of traveling the country with his wife, Ronnie Sue, in a motor home had been destroyed. They'd had to sell the motor home, and Ambrosino wanted Madoff to suffer, too. "As the guard who used to be on the right side of the prison bars, I'll know what Mr. Madoff's experience will be and will know that he is in prison in much the same way he imprisoned us as well as others," he said.

Madoff stared straight ahead or, at times, looked down at his hands in his lap or at the floor. He showed no emotion, although he seemed to be clenching his teeth.

A sixty-one-year-old widow, Maureen Ebel, described the emotional toll Madoff's crimes had taken on her as she was forced to take three jobs and sell the family home. "I had the horrible feeling that I had been pushed into the great black abyss," she said, referring to Madoff as a "psychopath."

Madoff was unmoved. This was the same man who

had not shed a tear when informed that two of his victims had committed suicide.

Others called him names: "evil low life," "a common thief." But neither the names nor the tears seemed to affect Madoff. He did not turn around to see who was speaking.

Carla Hirschhorn told the judge she and her husband had lost the money that was meant to pay for their daughter's college education, as the young woman sat two rows back dabbing at her tears.

"He killed my spirit and shattered my dreams," said former model Sharon Lissauer in a whispery voice.

Madoff had already been told by the judge that the nonbinding sentencing guidelines called for him to get a 150-year sentence. The former investors demanded he be shown no mercy.

Sixty-three-year-old Burt Ross broke down in tears twice and could not go on as he described the loss of the money that his father had worked so hard to save for his family. Ross said he had been taught that in each person there is "an inner light," but he could not find one in Madoff.

"Can we say Madoff was a righteous Jew who served on the boards of Jewish institutions when he sank so low," Ross began, and was again in tears and had to stop to regain his composure, with his wife holding him tight. "When he sank so low," he continued with gasps, "as to steal from Elie Wiesel, as if Wiesel hasn't already suffered enough in his lifetime. A righteous Jew, when in reality nobody has done more to reinforce the ugly stereotype that all we care about is money, despite the fact there are no people on this earth more charitable?"

The final victim to condemn Madoff was Cheryl Weinstein, who said she had met him when she served as the chief financial officer for Hadassah, a Jewish women's charitable organization. "I now view that day as perhaps the unluckiest day of my life," she told Judge Chin.

Eleanor Squillari remembered that Cheryl Weinstein was a frequent caller to Bernie over the years. "He would always roll his eyes when she called."

Weinstein described how she and her husband had been forced to sell the family home because of their losses. "I felt it was important for somebody who is personally acquainted with Madoff to speak," she said. "He is a beast that has stolen for his own needs the livelihoods, savings, lives, hopes and dreams, and futures of others in total disregard. He has fed upon us to satisfy his own needs. You should protect society from the likes of him," she urged the judge.

Weinstein later published a full account of her long extra-marital affair with Madoff, something she failed to mention during her dramatic courtroom testimony.

The cumulative weight of the denunciations from Madoff's once trusting investors was overwhelming, and efforts by his lawyer, Sorkin, to counter them failed miserably. "We cannot be unmoved by what we heard," said

Sorkin of the victims' accounts. "No doubt, we represent a deeply flawed individual."

In a letter to the judge a week earlier, Sorkin had called into question the motives of the victims. "We believe that the unified tone of the victim statements suggests a desire for a type of mob vengeance," he wrote.

Now on his feet, the veteran defense lawyer tried another tack, suggesting that the size of Madoff's crime had been grossly exaggerated by the news media, ignoring the fact that it was Madoff who initially set the total amount of fraud at $50 billion.

"The frenzy, the media excitement, that Mr. Madoff engaged in a Ponzi scheme involving $65 billion and that he has ferreted money away, as far as we know, Your Honor, that is simply not true," asserted Sorkin. The $65 billion figure was the amount Madoff's investors believed they had lost, based on the cumulative total of their last monthly statements. The government agreed that the actual amount of cash invested by investors between 1985 and 2008 was about $13 billion. Any amount beyond that represented the fake profits Madoff led his victims to believe they had earned.

Sorkin argued that much of the lost $13 billion might be recovered, suggesting that maybe Madoff wasn't all that bad. Sorkin pointed out that he had not tried to flee, and he and his family had also suffered "an enormous toll." Given Madoff's thirteen-year life expectancy, Sorkin thought a twelve-year sentence would be fair.

"We ask only, Your Honor, that Mr. Madoff be given understanding and fairness, within the parameters of our legal system, and that the sentence that he be given be sufficient, but not greater than necessary, to carry out what this court must carry out under the rules, statutes, and guidelines."

Madoff barely stirred as his lawyer spoke on his behalf. Sorkin's delivery seemed flat. He had been dealt a losing hand from the very beginning of the case. First, Madoff had essentially turned himself in to the FBI without consulting Sorkin. Then, he had given a lengthy, though largely untrue, statement to the FBI without consulting him. Again and again, Madoff had been a difficult client who seemed to think he was smarter than his own lawyer. It wasn't even clear if Sorkin's firm would be paid much more than the initial $250,000 he received from Madoff.

As a consummate professional, however, Sorkin tried to fashion a cogent argument that would have some resonance with the judge. For the sake of future business, at least, he had to be seen as giving it a shot.

"Mr. Madoff, if you would like to speak, now is the time," said Judge Chin.

Madoff stood up, holding his folded handwritten statement in front of him. His shirt collars now jutted outside his suit jacket, but he had given up any effort to tuck them in. It was over.

"Your Honor," Madoff started and then stopped. His voice was too dry to go on. He sipped from a glass of water. "Your Honor, I cannot offer you an excuse for my behavior," said Madoff, who three months earlier in his guilty plea had offered the excuse that his clients had pushed him to achieve impossible rates of return.

Another sip of water.

"How do you excuse betraying thousands of investors who entrusted me with their life savings?" Madoff said, trying his best to show some kind of remorse. At least he was no longer blaming the victims.

Then came the words that mattered most to him, as he again tried to deflect any blame or suspicion from his employees and his family. He knew his fate. This was his last chance to help others who were now under suspicion. "How do you excuse deceiving two hundred employees who have spent most of their working life working for me?" Lawyers for Frank DiPascali, Annette Bongiorno, and others who had worked on the seventeenth floor would appreciate that.

"How do you excuse lying to your brother and two sons who spent their whole adult life helping to build a successful and respectful business?" Madoff was back to the original version of his script that involved his confession to his brother and sons and then the FBI arrest. Andy and Mark might be behaving terribly toward their mother, but he was not going to throw them under the FBI bus.

"How do you excuse lying and deceiving a wife who stood by you for fifty years, and still stands by you?" Ruth was not there to hear the words, but she had already been told what Bernie would say. He told the judge that she would issue her own statement, part of a coordinated approach in which she would echo what Bernie said by announcing her own remorse. Everyone stayed on script.

To some reporters in the jury box, Madoff's most heartfelt words seem to come as he said he was sorry for bringing disgrace on the securities industry. "How do you excuse deceiving an industry that you spent a better part of your life trying to improve? There is no excuse for that, and I don't ask for forgiveness." It seemed the one part of his statement that he read with true conviction. Lawyers for all feeder funds would find good use for those words as they continued to proclaim their clients' innocence of any wrongdoing in their dealings with Madoff. They had been deceived by the master. If the SEC and the FBI had been fooled, how could they be expected to know better?

Madoff did not apologize for repeatedly lying to the SEC, but he went on to offer another explanation for his behavior. "I made an error of judgment. I refused to accept the fact, could not accept the fact, that for once in my life I failed. I couldn't admit that failure and that was a tragic mistake." This version of events seemed to imply that he had once been wildly and legitimately successful and then made one terrible mistake. Given his criminal, antisocial personality, the crime profilers had predicted this would be Madoff's explanation.

"The real key is that they believe they haven't done anything wrong," said former FBI agent Brad Garrett. "It is like narcissism on a scale that wouldn't fit in this room."

Madoff continued to read in a flat, almost hoarse voice. "People have accused me of being silent and not being sympathetic. That is not true," said Madoff as he neared the grand, theatrical climax of his statement to the judge. "They have accused my wife of being silent and not being sympathetic. Nothing could be further from the truth. She cries herself to sleep every night knowing of all the pain and suffering I have caused, and I am tormented by that as well."

Many of the victims wondered why he had waited until this moment to express his sympathy. He had been facing Judge Chin, with his back to them in the courtroom.

"I apologize to my victims," he read as he then announced his next move. "I will turn and face you." And he did. "I am sorry," he said. "I know that doesn't help you." And just as quickly he turned his back to them again. He had looked at the large group of victims no more than three or four seconds, with a stare that seemed to be focused on the back wood-paneled wall of the courtroom. He didn't make eye contact with any of them.

"Your Honor, thank you for listening to me."

The victims in the courtroom were unimpressed with his statement and his quick pivot to face them and apologize. "Pathetic," said Burt Ross. "It rings so hollow. I think it's very insincere," said Maureen Ebel, who was in the front row. "He did it perfunctorily and he just did it to help his case," said another victim, Jeff Shankman, who had once worked on the Madoff seventeenth floor and socialized with him and his family.

Lead prosecutor Lisa Baroni was short and to the point in underscoring why the government sought the maximum 150-year sentence. "This was not a crime born of any financial distress or market pressures," she said, contradicting Madoff's version that he was forced to cover up a onetime failure. "It was a calculated, well-orchestrated, long-term fraud carried out month after month, year after year, decade after decade."

Baroni made sure to address Sorkin's contention that Madoff should get some credit for turning himself in and not fleeing. "The defendant continued his fraud scheme until the very end, when he knew the scheme was days away from collapse and when he was faced with redemption requests from clients he knew he could not meet." Without saying it in so many words, Baroni made sure the judge knew the con man was still a man of deceit even after he turned himself in.

"The government respectfully requests that the court sentence the defendant to one hundred fifty years in prison or a substantial term of imprisonment that ensures that he will spend the rest of his life in jail," she concluded.

Judge Chin appeared to agree, but before he passed sentence he took the time to destroy any vestige of credibility left in the arguments made by Madoff and Sorkin.

"Despite all the emotion in the air, I do not agree with the suggestion that victims and others are seeking mob vengeance," said Judge Chin, going out of his way to criticize Sorkin's claim that the victims were somehow orchestrated or undeserving. "Objectively speaking, the fraud here was staggering."

"As many of the victims have pointed out, this is not just a matter of money. The breach of trust was massive," the judge said, as he went through a point-by-point rebuttal of Sorkin and Madoff. They did not win a single point in this debate.

"It is true that Mr. Madoff used much of the money to pay back investors who asked along the way to withdraw their accounts. But large sums were also taken by him, for his personal use and the use of his family, friends, and colleagues." And the judge then cited the money for the credit card purchases, the country club memberships, two yachts, and "the purchase of a Manhattan apartment for a relative." Madoff's vaunted generosity to his family—with stolen money—was now a guarantee he would spend life in prison.

Judge Chin said other arguments on Madoff's behalf "are less than compelling." He was unimpressed that Madoff "essentially turned himself in" because he knew "he was going to be caught soon." As to Sorkin's claim that Madoff had cooperated with the SEC by meeting with the inspector general for three hours, Judge Chin concluded, "I simply do not get the sense that Mr. Madoff has done all that he could or told all that he knows." The investigators and prosecutors in the room certainly knew that. They expected to spend at least another year trying to unravel the criminal conspiracy that Madoff had refused to describe.

Finally, the judge explained why he was prepared to order a sentence that would be "largely, if not entirely, symbolic" given Madoff's thirteen-year life expectancy. "Symbolism is important," he said. "Here the message must be sent that Mr. Madoff's crimes were extraordinarily evil, and this kind of irresponsible manipulation of the system is not merely a bloodless financial crime that takes place just on paper, but that it is instead, as we have heard, one that takes a staggering human toll."

In one final sharp poke in the eye of Sorkin, Judge Chin returned to the "mob vengeance" claim. "I do not agree that the victims are succumbing to the temptation of mob vengeance. Rather they are doing what they are supposed to be doing—placing their trust in our system of justice." If nothing else came out of the hearing, Sorkin and other members of the New York criminal defense bar now knew not to try the "mob vengeance" theme with Judge Chin again.

"Mr. Madoff, please stand. It is the judgment of this court that the defendant, Bernard L. Madoff, shall be and hereby is sentenced to a term of imprisonment of one hundred fifty years."

There were cheers and applause from the victims in

the courtroom. Many cried. Judge Chin did not order the courtroom to be silent.

"As a technical matter, the sentence must be expressed on the judgment in months. One hundred and fifty years is equivalent to eighteen hundred months."

Madoff barely blinked. He said nothing to his lawyers and did not turn around to face his victims. Four U.S. marshals were in place in case anyone tried to rush Madoff. As he was led away and rounded the jury box, a few of the reporters and sketch artists got a close look at his face. There were no tears in his eyes. In fact, at a point where he may have thought no one could see his face any longer, there was a little smile, a smirk, as his lips turned up and he nodded his head. Two weeks later, Madoff would be bused to his new and permanent home at the Butner Federal Correctional Institution in North Carolina. It was a medium security facility, just as Bernie had hoped for.

There was glee in the air outside as the victims emerged from the courthouse.

"He has truly earned the reputation for being the most despised American today," said Burt Ross.

Other victims scheduled a rally in front of the courthouse, where they turned their wrath toward the SEC, for failing to detect Madoff's scheme, and the bankruptcy trustee and the Securities Investor Protection Corporation (SIPC), for playing hardball in calculating how much the victims were owed.

One hour later, Ruth Madoff offered her own attack on Bernie, as she sought for the first time publicly to show she also had sympathy for the victims whose money had paid for her life of luxury.

"I am breaking my silence now, because my reluctance to speak has been interpreted as indifference or lack of sympathy for the victims of my husband Bernie's crime, which is exactly the opposite of the truth," read a written statement crafted with the help of her lawyer, Peter Chavkin.

"And in the days since December, I have read, with immense pain, the wrenching stories of people whose life savings have evaporated because of his crime." The expressions of sympathy did not include any apology, and the statement's more important purpose was to permit Ruth to declare she was not involved in any way in the scheme. "I am embarrassed and ashamed. Like everyone else, I feel betrayed and confused. The man who committed this horrible fraud is not the man whom I have known for all these years."

The statement also was a first step for Ruth in trying to reestablish her relationship with her sons, Mark and Andy, who had not spoken with her since their father's arrest. They considered her "an enabler." She wanted the boys to know she was not "an enabler" and had now joined the chorus of condemnation of their father.

Ruth did not appear in front of cameras to read the statement. She was too busy preparing to move out of the family home on East Sixty-fourth Street. Three days after her husband was sentenced, U.S. marshals arrived at the door of apartment 12-A and ordered Ruth to leave. She was denied permission to take her fur coat and left carrying only a straw bag.

Her deal with federal prosecutors did not preclude the SEC, the bankruptcy trustee, or any of the hundreds of private lawyers that represented the victims from acting against her in order to seek restitution. Ruth's $2.5 million was a small, but highly symbolic target.

She was unsure where to settle. Florida had laws that protected one's home from lawsuits, but it was also a place full of her husband's victims and painful reminders of her former life. Some people close to the family said they expected her to buy a small home near his prison in North Carolina. She was required to report any expenditure over $100 to the bankruptcy trustee, who remains suspicious that she and Bernie had hidden large amounts of cash somewhere.

Ruth still loved Bernie and wanted to continue seeing him and staying close as best she could as he spent the rest of his life in prison. She concluded that it was as if he had died but somehow she could still visit him. She told people close to her that, strangely, Bernie seemed much freer in prison than he had when he had all the fancy homes, the yachts, and the big bank accounts. He no longer had to worry about keeping his scheme going.

She said that it was as if every part of him had been compromised by the awful situation he got himself into.

Now he was spending his days listening to a radio she'd sent him and reading all those books he had not had the time for during his life as a criminal. He had added Coben and Forsyth to Grisham as his favorite authors. He would have time for a much more diverse list of authors.

Madoff appeared to be working out and looked "buff," according to one of his first visitors other than Ruth, San Francisco lawyer Joe Cotchett. Madoff appeared to be making himself at home and comfortable in North Carolina.

Even before she made her public statement, Ruth had talked with Bernie in prison about what he had done, about what they once had and what could have been. They had cried together. He had no tears for his victims, but he knew what he had lost and what he had done to Ruth. Their life together had been a fifty-year love story. The handsome suntanned lifeguard and the pretty blonde from Laurelton had been a perfect match. They had been just as happy running the business from a folding card table in their first apartment as when they had sleek offices in a Philip Johnson–designed building in Midtown Manhattan. The jet-set lifestyle was more than Ruth had ever hoped for.

Ruth told people close to her that she had not seen the end coming. In fact, a wonderful retirement had seemed around the corner for both of them. She said she believed Bernie's version of events, that he had been trapped in the scheme for decades and that he had not set out to be a crook. Bernie's wandering eye could be forgiven; Ruth told people she knew that Bernie never set out to hurt her. If she'd had her doubts over the years, as she balanced the books and offered advice on business strategy, she had not raised them. Not to Bernie, who was the one she and everyone she knew "respected and trusted with our lives and our livelihoods."

He had destroyed everything. In person with Bernie, Ruth was both sympathetic and forgiving. She was glad her husband had found a way to deal with prison life and she was comforted by the irony that he seemed so free behind bars. She told Bernie it reminded her of what could have been possible if he had not cheated so many, lied so grandly, and stolen so much.

Ruth told Bernie, "What a waste of a life."

Madoff Employees and Relatives Convicted of Crimes

THE TEAM OF CRIMINALS BEHIND BERNIE MADOFF

Case Name and Number	Defendant	Status
US v. Bernard Madoff (09 Cr. 213 DC)	Bernard Madoff	*Pled guilty on 3/12/2009 to an eleven-count Information charging him with securities fraud, investment advisor fraud, mail fraud, wire fraud, international money laundering, money laundering, making false statements, perjury, making false filings to the Securities and Exchange Commission, and theft from an employee benefit plan *Sentenced 6/29/09 to 150 years in prison
US v. David Friehling (09 Cr. 700 AKH)	David Friehling	*Pled guilty on 11/3/2009 to a nine-count Superseding Information charging him with securities fraud, investment adviser fraud, filing false audit reports with the United States Securities and Exchange Commission, and obstructing or impeding the administration of the internal revenue laws *Sentenced 5/28/15 to time served, two years supervised release, home detention for 10 months, 200 hours of community service, $130 billion forfeiture.
US v. Frank DiPascali (09 Cr. 764 RJS)	Frank DiPascali	*Pled guilty on 8/11/2009 to a ten-count Information charging him with conspiracy, securities fraud, investment adviser fraud, falsifying records of a broker-dealer, falsifying records of an investment adviser, mail fraud, wire fraud, international money laundering, perjury, and attempting to evade federal income taxes *Criminal forfeiture money judgment in the amount of $170.25 billion *Sentencing set for 9/10/2015. *Defendant died 5/9/2015.
US v. Jerome O'Hara, et al. (10 Cr. 228 LTS)	Jerome O'Hara	*Found guilty on 3/24/2014 after 5-month jury trial: conspiracy to defraud, conspiracy to commit securities fraud, securities fraud, falsifying records of a broker-dealer. * Sentenced 12/9/2014 to 30 months in prison and $19.7 billion forfeiture.
	George Perez	*Found guilty on 3/24/2014 after 5-month jury trial: conspiracy to defraud, conspiracy to commit securities fraud, securities fraud, falsifying records of a broker-dealer. * Sentenced 12/10/2014 to 30 months in prison, 3 years supervised release, $19.7 billion forfeiture.
	Daniel Bonventre	*Found guilty on 3/24/2014 after 5-month jury trial: conspiracy to defraud, conspiracy to commit securities fraud, conspiracy to commit accounting fraud, conspiracy to commit tax fraud, conspiracy to commit ERISA fraud, securities fraud, falsifying records, false filing with the SEC, bank fraud, subscribing to false U.S. income tax returns, corrupt or forcible interference. *Sentenced 12/8/2014 to 10 years in prison and $155 billion forfeiture

Annette Bongiorno	*Found guilty on 3/24/2014 after 5-month jury trial: conspiracy to defraud, securities fraud, falsifying records, attempt to evade or defeat tax, corrupt or forcible interference. * Sentenced 12/9/2014 to 6 years in prison, one year supervised release and $155 billion forfeiture.
Joann Crupi	*Found guilty on 3/24/2014 after 5-month jury trial: conspiracy to defraud Madoff securities, conspiracy to commit securities fraud, securities fraud, falsifying records, attempt and conspiracy to commit bank fraud, bank fraud, attempt to evade or defeat tax. * Sentenced 12/15/2014 to six years in prison, four years supervised release, and $37 billion forfeiture.
Eric Lipkin	*Pled guilty on 6/6/2011 to a six-count Superseding Information charging him with conspiracy, falsifying books and records of a broker-dealer, falsifying books and records of an investment advisor, bank fraud, and making false statements to facilitate a theft concerning the Employee Retirement Income Security Act * Agreed for forfeit at least $1.4 million * Sentenced 5/20/2015 to time served, two years supervised release, home detention of nine months, and $30 billion forfeiture.
David L. Kugel	*Pled guilty on 11/21/2011 to a six-count Superseding Information charging him with conspiracy, securities fraud, falsifying books and records of a broker-dealer, falsifying books and records of an investment adviser, and bank fraud. * Agreed for forfeit more than $170 billion, including his interests in homes, a luxury car, various accounts at financial institutions, and other specific assets. * Sentenced 5/27/2015 to time served, home detention for 10 months, two years supervised release, 200 hours of community service, and $170 billion forfeiture.
Enrica Cotellessa-Pitz	*Pled guilty on 12/19/2011 a four-count Superseding Information charging her with conspiracy, falsifying books and records of a broker-dealer, falsifying books and records of an investment adviser, and making false filings to the Securities and Exchange Commission. * Sentenced 5/27/2015 to two years served, two years supervised release, and $97 billion forfeiture.
Craig Kugel	*Pled guilty on 6/5/2012 to a five-count Superseding Information charging him with conspiracy, making false statements in relation to documents required by the Employee Retirement Income Security Act, and subscribing to false U.S. individual income tax returns. * At least $2.3 million in forfeiture * Sentenced 6/4/2015 to time served, two years supervised release, and $2 billion forfeiture.

(continued on p. 234)

	Irwin Lipkin	Pled guilty 11/8/2012 to a two-count Superseding Information charging him with conspiracy to commit securities fraud, to falsify records, to make false filings with the SEC, and to falsify statements in relation to documents required by ERISA, and one count of falsifying statements in relation to documents required by ERISA
	Peter Madoff	*Pled guilty on 6/29/2012 to a two-count Superseding Information charging him with conspiracy to commit Securities Fraud, falsify records of an investment adviser, falsifying records of a broker-dealer, making false filings with the SEC, committing mail fraud, falsifying statements in relation to documents required by ERISA, and obstructing and impeding the lawful governmental function of the IRS. * More than $143.1 billion, including all of his real and personal property * The surrendered assets include, among other things, several homes, a Ferrari and more than $10 million in cash and securities. Marion Madoff is being left with approximately $771,733 to live on for the rest of her life. *Sentenced on 12/20/2012 to 10 years in prison
US v. Paul Konigsberg (S11 10 Cr. 228 LTS)	Paul Konigsberg	*Charged 9/26/2013 for his role in the scheme to falsify books and records at Bernard L. Madoff Investment Securities, through which Bernard L. Madoff ran his multibillion-dollar Ponzi scheme. He was also charged in connection with his role in creating a fictitious, no-show job through which a co-conspirator received hundreds of thousands of dollars in compensation from Madoff. *Released on bail

APPENDIX

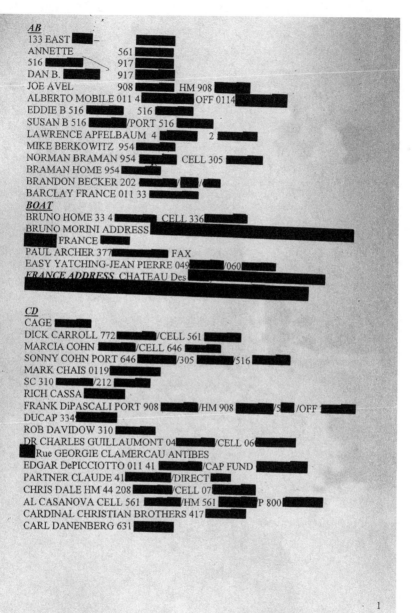

AB
133 EAST ▮▮ –   ▮▮▮
ANNETTE   561▮
516 ▮▮   917▮
DAN B. ▮▮   917▮
JOE AVEL   908▮▮   HM 908 ▮▮▮
ALBERTO MOBILE 011 4▮▮▮▮OFF 0114▮▮▮▮▮
EDDIE B 516 ▮▮▮   516 ▮▮▮
SUSAN B 516 ▮▮▮/PORT 516 ▮▮▮
LAWRENCE APFELBAUM 4 ▮▮▮   2 ▮▮▮▮
MIKE BERKOWITZ 954▮▮▮
NORMAN BRAMAN 954 ▮▮▮   CELL 305 ▮▮▮
BRAMAN HOME 954▮▮▮
BRANDON BECKER 202 ▮▮▮/▮/▮
BARCLAY FRANCE 011 33 ▮▮▮
BOAT
BRUNO HOME 33 4▮▮▮   CELL 336▮▮▮
BRUNO MORINI ADDRESS ▮▮▮▮▮
▮▮ FRANCE ▮▮
PAUL ARCHER 377▮▮▮ FAX
EASY YATCHING-JEAN PIERRE 049▮▮/060▮▮▮
FRANCE ADDRESS CHATEAU Des ▮▮▮▮▮
▮▮▮▮▮▮▮

CD
CAGE ▮▮▮
DICK CARROLL 772▮▮▮/CELL 561 ▮▮▮
MARCIA COHN ▮▮▮/CELL 646 ▮▮▮
SONNY COHN PORT 646▮▮▮/305 ▮▮▮/516 ▮▮▮
MARK CHAIS 0119▮▮▮
SC 310 ▮▮▮/212 ▮▮▮
RICH CASSA ▮▮▮
FRANK DiPASCALI PORT 908 ▮▮▮/HM 908 ▮▮▮/5▮ /OFF ▮▮▮
DUCAP 334▮
ROB DAVIDOW 310 ▮▮▮
DR CHARLES GUILLAUMONT 04▮▮▮/CELL 06▮▮
▮▮Rue GEORGIE CLAMERCAU ANTIBES
EDGAR DePICCIOTTO 011 41 ▮▮▮/CAP FUND ▮▮▮
PARTNER CLAUDE 41▮▮▮/DIRECT ▮▮
CHRIS DALE HM 44 208 ▮▮▮/CELL 07▮▮
AL CASANOVA CELL 561 ▮▮▮/HM 561 ▮▮▮P 800▮▮▮
CARDINAL CHRISTIAN BROTHERS 417▮▮▮
CARL DANENBERG 631 ▮▮▮

1

A. Bernie Madoff's "little black book" of what he deemed his essential contacts contained 151 names, ranging from his housekeeper in France, to his investors and victims, to his inner circle on the seventeenth floor. His secretary, Eleanor, typed an annual version in case he lost the book. She provided it to the FBI and the author.

EF
ELEANOR/718 ███████ ELAINE 212 ███████
ERROL 917 ███████
FABIAN 06 ███████
AHMED 441 ████ (FAIR) CELL 646 ███████/917 ███████
JEROME FISHER 561 ████████/561 ████████/PORT 561 ███████
KEVIN FONG 201 ███████
MANUEL ECHEVERRA 0114 ████████/7██ DIRECT/FAX 0114 ███████
CELL 0114 ███████
(FAIR)MARK McKEEFRY 212 ███████/CELL 917 ███████
FISHER ISLAND 305 ███████
LEON FLAX 01144 ████████/PORT 01144 ███████
DAVID FREIHLING HM 845 ████████FAX/CELL 845 ███████
OFF 845 ████████/ADDRESS ███████
STEVE FITT OFF 612 ████████/HM 612 ███████
MURRAY EISEN 516 ███████
CAROL EISEN 516 ███████
CHARLES FIX 0114 ████████0114 ███████
FED-EX 108 ███████

GH
GROSSO CELL 447 ████████/HM 441 ████████/NY OFF 212 ███████
HSBC PAUL SMITH 212 ███████
R. GLANTZ 415 ████████/HM 415 ███████
YAIR GREEN HM 0119 ████████/OFF ███████
YAIR GREEN TEL AVIV 0119 ████████/CELL 0119 ███████
CERETTI 44 ████████/PORT 443 ███████
J.HOROWITZ 561 ███████
JOE HARDIMAN 561 ████████/410 ████████/410 ███████
IRA HARRIS ███████

IJ
JULIETTE 561 ███████
JODI 908 ████████/CELL 917 ████████DAD 702 ███████
JON JENNERET 315 ████████/HM 315 ███████
BOB JAFFE 617 ████████CELL
JEAN-RECEPTION HM 646 ████████/CELL 646 ███████
EUROJET ITALIA 02 ████████/FAX 0 ███████
JACK EADES 954 ███████

KL
ERIC LIPKIN 201 ████████/917 ███████
FRANKIE D HM 845 ████████/CELL 845 ███████
CRAIG KUGEL 917 ███████
KPMG DAVID YIM 442 ████████/OFF 44 2 ███████
MOBILE 44(0) ███████

2

LAGOON/LAURENT MATHERSON GURST 41 22 ███████
LATIS FAMILY (GREEK) EFG GROUP
LEE 914 ███████/HM
STEVE KRASS ███████
HARVEY KRAUSS ███████
KARYO 049 ███████/CELL 06███████
SAUL KATZ 516 ███████CELL 516 ███████/561 ███████
PIAGE KELLER 04███████
PAUL K 685 ███████/HM 212 ███████/PORT 917 ███████/203 ███████
FL HOUSE 561 ███████
LANESBOROUGH ███████
LONDON TAXI ███████ ACC# 46███
PATRICK LITTAYE PORT 324███████
FRANK LEVY HM ███████/CELL 917 ███████

_MN_

TERRY ███████/███/CELL 908 ███████
PETER NEEDHAM 631 ███████
JOHN @MARINA ███████
MAYO CLINIC EMERGENCY NETJET/507 ███████
MURIEL/CELL 33 ███████/FAX ███████
MIKE MACRIOLI 202 ███████
NYYC # M1██
B MADF APT FAX ███████
B MARDEN 561 ███████/212 ███████
RICHARD MALTZ 914███████
S MENDELOW 212 ███████
NANDO PIGNATELLI 003 ███████
WALTER NOEL HM 203 ███████
STEPHANIE MADOFF 917 ███████
LEANA 516 ███████/631 ███████
LENA 347 ███████
SHARON 212 ███████
BRENDA CLARIC 646 ███████
HEATHER 516 ███████
LISA 917 ███████
CAROLE 062███████
MARIE 066███████
RICK MORALES 954 ███████
BEACH POLICE 049███████
SHARON PB MASSAGE 561 ███████
PBM PB FAX 561 ███████
JOHN PINTO 202 ███████
TOM PRITCHARD 917███████

3

J PICOWER 561 ███
APRIL 914 ███ /CELL 914 ███
LEE PICARD 202 ███
MARYANN PISSARI/ CRAIG LANDAUER 202 ███
FRANK PETITO ███ /HM ███
ELAINE PIKULIK 718 ███
DR. POST 212 ███ /516 ███
POST 212 ███ /PRIVATE 212 ███
PLAZA 01133 ███
PARK LANE 077 ███
OPTIMAL /JON CLARK 212 ███
PB POLICE 561 ███
VOLK ███ /CELL ███ /BEEP ███
BELACE ███
FIBRE SEAL ███ ███
PORT GALLICE BD BAUDOUIN, ███

PIERRE PRADIE 01133 ███ / ███ ███ PARIS

OR

RECEPTION-JEAN LARSEN HM 6 ███ /CELL 646 ███

ARTHUR ROCK 415 ███
S. RAVEN 01144 ███ / CELL 44 ███ /SPAIN ███ PORT

ST
SS#069 ███
BANQUE SAFRA – JOE HABBORBA 331 ███
MALCOLM STEVENGO 01144 ███
ADAM STRACHER 917 ███
HSBC PAUL SMITH 212 ███ /CELL 917 ███
ERIC M.G. SYZ 41 ███
SCOTT SOSNIK 201 ███
BOB SCHULMAN 914 ███ CELL/OFF 914 ███
DICK SPRING 561 ███ / ███ ../CELL 561 ███ &516 ███
BOB SCHOR ███
C.S. 561 ███ &617 ███ / ███
TERRY McDONNELL 732 ███
RON TAVLIN 612 ███
JEFF TUCKER DIRECT 212 ███ /CELL 518 ███
WALTER TITLENICK ███
(SHOESLOBB ███

UVW
VIP ANGELA   CELL61 ███ OFF 01133 ███

4

FRED WILPON 516 /212 ████/561 ████
CHARLES WIENER 631 ████
WESTPORT BANK & TRUST/BOB SILVERMAN 203 ████/HM 203 ████
VIEN 631 ████
VILLA 049 ████
MIKE WOLK 202 ████/CELL 240 ████

_YZ_

ALAN YASNI 818 ████
SUSAN YOUNG ASSIST TO J LEVY
OFFICE 212 ████

SEC DIVISION OF ENFORCEMENT
Case Opening Report

Run on 1/24/2006

Case No.: NY-07563   **Case Name:**   Certain Hedge Fund Trading Pr

Date Opened: 1/4/2006

Case Opening Narrative:

The staff received a complaint alleging that Bernard L. Madoff Investment Securities LLC, a registered broker-dealer in New York ("BLM"), operates an undisclosed multi-billion dollar investment advisory business, and that BLM operates this business as a Ponzi scheme. The complaint did not contain specific facts about the alleged Ponzi scheme, and the complainant was neither a BLM insider nor an aggrieved investor. Nevertheless, because of the substantial amounts at issue, the staff, in the abundance of caution, requested voluntary production of certain documents from BLM and two of its hedge fund customers, Fairfield Sentry Limited and Greenwich Sentry, L.P., affiliates of the New York-based Fairfield Greenwich Group ("FGG") (collectively, the "Sentry Funds"). The staff also conducted a voluntary interview of an FGG officer. The staff found, first, that neither BLM nor the Sentry Funds disclose to investors that the investment decisions for the Sentry Funds are made by BLM rather than by FGG, and that, in substance, BLM acts as an undisclosed investment adviser to the Sentry Funds. Second, the staff found that, during an SEC examination of BLM that was conducted earlier this year, BLM – and more specifically, its principal Bernard L. Madoff, – mislead the examination staff about the nature of the strategy implemented in the Sentry Funds' and certain other hedge fund customers' accounts, and also withheld from the examination staff information about certain of these customers' accounts at BLM. Third, the evidence obtained so far suggests that BLM also acts as an undisclosed investment adviser to several additional hedge funds.

The staff is now seeking additional evidence, in the form of documents and witness testimony from BLM and its hedge fund customers, on the issues of BLM's role in those hedge funds' investment activities and the adequacy of related disclosures. Additionally, the staff is trying to ascertain whether the complainant's allegation that BLM is operating a Ponzi scheme has any factual basis.

Signatures:

[signature]
Attorney   1/24/06
                                                                  Date

[signature]
Branch Chief   1/24/06
                                                                  Date

[signature] Bache-heimer
Asst Dir/Asst Reg Adm/Dist Adm   1/24/06
                                                                  Date

---

Submit this form to the Office of Chief Counsel, Division of Enforcement.

B. SEC investigators prepared an "opening narrative" in early 2006 when they finally decided to investigate allegations from Harry Markopolos that Bernie Madoff was running the world's biggest Ponzi scheme.

SEC DIVISION OF ENFORCEMENT
Case Closing Recommendation

Run on 11/21/2007

Case No.: NY-07563   **Case Name:** Certain Hedge Fund Trading Pra

Case Closing Recommendation Narrative:

Investigation Closing Narrative

NY-7563/Certain Hedge Fund Trading Practices

I.☐Reason Opened:

The staff opened this case on January 4, 2006, to investigate (1) whether Bernard L. Madoff Investment Securities LLC ("BLM"), a registered broker-dealer, provided investment advisory services to large hedge funds in violation of the registration requirements of the Investment Advisers Act of 1940, and (2) whether BLM engaged in any fraudulent activities in connection with these services. The investigation was prompted, first, by a letter from an "independent fraud investigator," a person who had previously provided helpful information to the enforcement staff at BDO, alleging that the returns reported by BLM's hedge fund clients were the result of fraud perpetrated by BLM. Second, in the course of a preliminary inquiry into these allegations, the staff learned that, during a recent examination of BLM by NERO's broker-dealer examination staff, Bernard Madoff, the sole owner of BLM, did not fully disclose to the examination staff either the nature of the trading conducted in the hedge fund accounts or the number of such accounts at BLM.

II.☐Work Performed:

BLM and two of its largest hedge fund clients voluntarily produced documents to the staff. The staff took the voluntary testimony of Bernard Madoff, his assistant, and a principal of BLM's largest hedge fund client, Fairfield Greenwich Group ("FGG"). The staff also interviewed a FGG employee.

III.☐Conclusions Reached:

The staff found no evidence of fraud. The staff did find, however, that BLM acted as an investment adviser to certain hedge funds, institutions and high net worth individuals in violation of the registration requirements of the Advisers Act. The staff also found that FGG's disclosures to its investors did not adequately describe BLM's advisory role and described BLM as merely an executing broker to FGG's accounts. As a result of discussions with the staff, BLM registered with the Commission as an investment adviser, and FGG revised its disclosures to investors to reflect BLM's advisory role.

IV.☐Reasons for Closing:

We recommend closing this investigation because both BLM and FGG voluntarily remedied the uncovered violations, and because those violations were not so serious as to warrant an enforcement action.

V.☐Compliance Requirements:

☐All files have been prepared for closing in accordance with the procedures set forth in the McLucas and Butler memorandum dated August 20th, 1993, concerning the disposition of records upon the closing of cases. No access requests or protective orders governing the case records are outstanding. According to the Commission's FOIA office, as of January 10, 2007, the most recent denial of a FOIA request (request number 07-01646-FOIA) in this matter was on January 3, 2007. The request remains a FOIA concern as the requester has six years to appeal the denial. Accordingly, any materials the staff is not otherwise required to retain will be retained upon closing as Category F records. There are no Category E records. Termination letters have been sent to Bernard L. Madoff Investment Securities LLC, Bernard L. Madoff, and Fairfield Greenwich Group. The staff has no objection to the eventual destruction of the files and has no knowledge of any impediment to such a disposition.

VI.☐Names and Titles of Staff:

☐This closing recommendation was prepared by Simona Suh, Staff Attorney, and reviewed and approved by Doria Bachenheimer, Assistant Regional Director, and Meaghan Cheung, Branch Chief.

Representations

A.   FOIA

After consultation with FOIA/PA Branch, it was determined that the FOIA status of these case files is as follows (Check one):

☐ No FOIA concerns exist as of _____ .

☐ FOIA request filed on _____ is pending without decision. Category F Material will be retired with balance of file.

☐ FOIA request was denied on _____ . Category F Material will be marked to be discarded six years after decision date.

☐ FOIA determination was appealed and decided on _____ . Category F Material will be marked to be discarded six years after decision date.

B.   Category E Records

☐ The files contain no Category E Records.

☐ A copy of the index for all designated Category E (Miscellaneous) Records is attached.

C.   Termination Letters

☐ No termination letters are required.

☐ Termination letters will be sent to the parties listed in the case narrative.

C. SEC investigators closed out their investigation of Bernie Madoff's alleged Ponzi scheme with a finding of "no evidence of fraud" in a closing.

FORM **1040X**	Department of the Treasury–Internal Revenue Service		OMB No. 1545-1074
Rev. November 2007	**Amended U.S. Individual Income Tax Return** ▶ See separate instructions.		

This return is for calendar year ▶ **2007** , or fiscal year ended ▶

Your first name and initial	Last name	Your social security number
BERNARD L.	**MADOFF**	
If a joint return, spouse's first name and initial	Last name	Spouse's social security number
RUTH	**MADOFF**	

Home address (no. and street) or P.O. box if mail is not delivered to your home   Apt. no.   Phone number
133 EAST 64TH STREET

City, town or post office, state, and ZIP code. If you have a foreign address, see page 3 of the instructions.
NEW YORK   **NY 10021**

☐COPY

A If the address shown above is different from that shown on your last return filed with the IRS, would you like us to change it in our records? ▶ ☐ Yes ☐ No

B Filing status. Be sure to complete this line. Note. You cannot change from joint to separate returns after the due date.
On original return ▶ ☐ Single ☒ Married filing jointly ☐ Married filing separately ☐ Head of household* ☐ Qualifying widow(er)
On this return ▶ ☐ Single ☒ Married filing jointly ☐ Married filing separately ☐ Head of household* ☐ Qualifying widow(er)
* If the qualifying person is a child but not your dependent, see page 3 of the instructions.

	Use Part II on the back to explain any changes		A. Original amount or as previously adjusted (see page 3)	B. Net change—amount of increase or (decrease)—explain in Part II	C. Correct amount
	Income and Deductions (see instructions)				
1	Adjusted gross income (see page 3)	1	13,261,071	1,635	13,262,706
2	Itemized deductions or standard deduction (see page 4)	2	8,055,157	784	8,055,941
3	Subtract line 2 from line 1	3	5,205,914	851	5,206,765
4	Exemptions. If changing, fill in Parts I and II on the back (see page 4)	4	2,266		2,266
5	Taxable income. Subtract line 4 from line 3	5	5,203,648	851	5,204,499
6	Tax (see page 5). Method used in col. C **Sch. D**	6	1,775,916	229	1,776,145
7	Credits (see page 5)	7	818,780		818,780
8	Subtract line 7 from line 6. Enter the result but not less than zero	8	957,136	229	957,365
9	Other taxes (see page 6)	9	264,432		264,432
10	Total tax. Add lines 8 and 9	10	1,221,568	229	1,221,797
11	Federal income tax withheld and excess social security and tier 1 RRTA tax withheld. If changing, see page 5	11	28		28
12	Estimated tax payments, including amount applied from prior year's return	12	0		
13	Earned income credit (EIC)	13	0		
14	Additional child tax credit from Form 8812	14	0		
15	Credits: Federal telephone excise tax or from Forms 2439, 4136, 8885, or 8801 (if refundable)	15	0		
16	Amount paid with request for extension of time to file (see page 5)			16	1,900,000
17	Amount of tax paid with original return plus additional tax paid after it was filed			17	
18	Total payments. Add lines 11 through 17 in column C			18	1,900,028

Refund or Amount You Owe

19	Overpayment, if any, as shown on original return or as previously adjusted by the IRS			19	678,460
20	Subtract line 19 from line 18 (see page 6)			20	1,221,568
21	Amount you owe. If line 10, column C, is more than line 20, enter the difference and see page 6			21	229
22	If line 10, column C, is less than line 20, enter the difference			22	
23	Amount of line 22 you want refunded to you			23	
24	Amount of line 22 you want applied to your estimated tax ▶	24			

Sign Here
Joint return?
See page 2.
Keep a copy for your records.

Under penalties of perjury, I declare that I have filed an original return and that I have examined this amended return, including accompanying schedules and statements, and to the best of my knowledge and belief, this amended return is true, correct, and complete. Declaration of preparer (other than taxpayer) is based on all information of which the preparer has any knowledge.

| ▶ Your signature   Date | ▶ Spouse's signature. If a joint return, both must sign.   Date |

Paid Preparer's Use Only

| Preparer's signature | **David G. Friehling** | Date **10/29/08** | Check if self-employed ☐ | Preparer's SSN or PTIN |
| Firm's name (or yours if self-employed), address, and ZIP code | **Friehling & Horowitz, CPA's P.C.** **337 N Main St** **New City, NY 10956** | | EIN | Phone no. **845-639-0501** |

For Paperwork Reduction Act Notice, see page 7 of instructions.   Form **1040X** (Rev. 11-2007)
DAA

D. In the last federal tax return they would file before Madoff's scheme collapsed, Bernie and Ruth reported an income of $9,422,238.

BERNARD L. & RUTH MADOFF

Form 1040X (Rev. 11-2007)   Page 2

Exemptions. See Form 1040 or 1040A instructions.

Complete this part only if you are:
- Increasing or decreasing the number of exemptions claimed on line 6d of the return you are amending, or
- Increasing or decreasing the exemption amount for housing individuals displaced by Hurricane Katrina.

		A. Original number of exemptions reported or as previously adjusted	B. Net change	C. Correct number of exemptions
25	Yourself and spouse	25		
	Caution. If someone can claim you as a dependent, you cannot claim an exemption for yourself.			
26	Your dependent children who lived with you	26		
27	Your dependent children who did not live with you due to divorce or separation	27		
28	Other dependents	28		
29	Total number of exemptions. Add lines 25 through 28	29		
30	Multiply the number of exemptions claimed on line 29 by the amount listed below for the tax year you are amending. Enter the result here.	30		
31	If you are claiming an exemption amount for housing individuals displaced by Hurricane Katrina, enter the amount from Form 8914, line 2 for 2005 or line 6 for 2006 (see instructions for line 4). Otherwise enter -0-.	31		
32	Add lines 30 and 31. Enter the result here and on line 4	32		

But see the instructions for line 4 on page 3 if the amount on line 1 is over:

Tax year	Exemption amount	
2007	$3,400	$117,300
2006	3,300	112,875
2005	3,200	109,475
2004	3,100	107,025

33 Dependents (children and other) not claimed on original (or adjusted) return:

(A) First name Last name	(b) Dependent's social security number	(c) Dependent's relationship to you	(d) ✔ if qualifying child for child tax credit (see page 6)	No. of children on 33 who:
				● lived with you .... ☐
				● did not live with you due to divorce or separation (see page 6) ...... ☐
				Dependents on 33 not entered above ☐

Explanation of Changes

Enter the line number from the front of the form for each item you are changing and give the reason for each change. Attach only the supporting forms and schedules for the items changed. If you do not attach the required information, your Form 1040X may be returned. Be sure to include your name and social security number on any attachments.

If the change relates to a net operating loss carryback or a general business credit carryback, attach the schedule or form that shows the year in which the loss or credit occurred. See page 2 of the instructions. Also, check here ▶ ☐

Taxpayer's spouse receive a K-1 from New Jersey MR Imaging aafter the original 1040 was efiled. This accounts for the additional tax due.

Presidential Election Campaign Fund. Checking below will not increase your tax or reduce your refund.

If you did not previously want $3 to go to the fund but now want to, check here ▶ ☐
If a joint return and your spouse did not previously want $3 to go to the fund but now wants to, check here ▶ ☐

Form **1040X** (Rev. 11-2007)

DAA

Form **1040**	Department of the Treasury—Internal Revenue Service **U.S. Individual Income Tax Return**	**2007**	(99)	IRS Use Only—Do not write or staple in this space.

For the year Jan. 1–Dec. 31, 2007, or other tax year beginning _____, 2007, ending _____, 20___   OMB No. 1545-0074

Label
(See instructions on page 12.)
Use the IRS label.
Otherwise, please print or type.

Your first name and initial	Last name	Your social security number
BERNARD L.	MADOFF	[redacted]
If a joint return, spouse's first name and initial	Last name	Spouse's social security number
RUTH	MADOFF	[redacted]

Home address (number and street). If you have a P.O. box, see page 12.   Apt. no.
133 EAST 64TH STREET

City, town or post office, state, and ZIP code. If you have a foreign address, see page 12.
NEW YORK   NY 10021

You must enter your SSN(s) above. ▲

Presidential Election Campaign ▶ Check here if you, or your spouse if filing jointly, want $3 to go to this fund (see page 12) ▶   [X] You   [X] Spouse

Checking a box below will not change your tax or refund.

Filing Status
Check only one box.

1 ☐ Single
2 [X] Married filing jointly (even if only one had income)
3 ☐ Married filing separately. Enter spouse's SSN above and full name here. ▶
4 ☐ Head of household (with qualifying person). (See page 13.) If the qualifying person is a child but not your dependent, enter this child's name here. ▶
5 ☐ Qualifying widow(er) with dependent child (see page 14)

Exemptions

6a [X] Yourself. If someone can claim you as a dependent, do not check box 6a
b [X] Spouse

Boxes checked on 6a and 6b   **2**

c Dependents:

(1) First name Last name	(2) Dependent's social security number	(3) Dependent's relationship to you	(4) ✓ if qualifying child for child tax credit (see page 15)

If more than four dependents, see page 15.

No. of children on 6c who:
• lived with you
• did not live with you due to divorce or separation (see page 16)
Dependents on 6c not entered above

d Total number of exemptions claimed   Add numbers on lines above ▶   **2**

Income

Attach Form(s) W-2 here. Also attach Forms W-2G and 1099-R if tax was withheld.

If you did not get a W-2, see page 19.

Enclose, but do not attach, any payment. Also, please use Form 1040-V.

7	Wages, salaries, tips, etc. Attach Form(s) W-2	7	3,679,311
8a	Taxable interest. Attach Schedule B if required	8a	
b	Tax-exempt interest. Do not include on line 8a	8b 2,566,428	
9a	Ordinary dividends. Attach Schedule B if required	9a	120,067
b	Qualified dividends (see page 19)	9b 54,960	
10	Taxable refunds, credits, or offsets of state and local income taxes (see page 20)	10	
11	Alimony received	11	
12	Business income or (loss). Attach Schedule C or C-EZ	12	9,422,238
13	Capital gain or (loss). Attach Schedule D if required. If not required, check here ▶ ☐	13	1,355,808
14	Other gains or (losses). Attach Form 4797	14	
15a	IRA distributions 15a _____ b Taxable amount (see page 21)	15b	
16a	Pensions and annuities 16a _____ b Taxable amount (see page 22)	16b	
17	Rental real estate, royalties, partnerships, S corporations, trusts, etc. Attach Schedule E	17	-1,183,502
18	Farm income or (loss). Attach Schedule F	18	
19	Unemployment compensation	19	
20a	Social security benefits 20a _____ b Taxable amount (see page 24)	20b	
21	Other income. List type and amount (see page 24)	21	
22	Add the amounts in the far right column for lines 7 through 21. This is your **total income** ▶	22	13,394,922

Adjusted Gross Income

23	Educator expenses (see page 26)	23	
24	Certain business expenses of reservists, performing artists, and fee-basis government officials. Attach Form 2106 or 2106-EZ	24	
25	Health savings account deduction. Attach Form 8889	25	
26	Moving expenses. Attach Form 3903	26	
27	One-half of self-employment tax. Attach Schedule SE	27 132,216	
28	Self-employed SEP, SIMPLE, and qualified plans	28	
29	Self-employed health insurance deduction (see page 26)	29	
30	Penalty on early withdrawal of savings	30	
31a	Alimony paid b Recipient's SSN ▶	31a	
32	IRA deduction (see page 27)	32	
33	Student loan interest deduction (see page 30)	33	
34	Tuition and fees deduction. Attach Form 8917	34	
35	Domestic production activities deduction. Attach Form 8903	35	
36	Add lines 23 through 31a and 32 through 35	36	132,216
37	Subtract line 36 from line 22. This is your **adjusted gross income** ▶	37	13,262,706

For Disclosure, Privacy Act, and Paperwork Reduction Act Notice, see page 83.
DAA

Form **1040** (2007)

NOTES

The information in this book is based on dozens of interviews, documents filed in court, records and files from inside the Madoff offices, and the extensive reporting of the ABC News investigative unit. Given the sensitivity of the ongoing criminal investigations and civil lawsuits, many of the people who were interviewed did so only on the condition that their names would not be used. Bernie and Ruth lived in a world full of secrets and they confided in few people. Some of those few felt it important that the Madoffs' story be told because of the enormity of the crime and the complexity of assigning guilt, including people who spoke in defense of Ruth and the two Madoff sons, Mark and Andrew.

CHAPTER ONE

2 *Instead of a day:* Ira Sorkin
2 *"do the right thing":* Person close to Mark and Andrew Madoff
2 *He had asked his sons:* Person close to Mark and Andrew Madoff
2 *Madoff, a meticulous:* Law enforcement sources

2   *"an innocent explanation"*: USA v. Bernard L. Madoff, Complaint, December 11, 2008

4   *At the time of:* Irving Picard

5   *Whatever it was that Sorkin:* Person familiar with Bernard Madoff

7   *Within days, Madoff:* Person familiar with Bernard Madoff

8   *He believed he could "sell":* Person familiar with Bernard Madoff

8   *"there will be a life after this":* Person familiar with Bernard Madoff

8   *Prosecutors later admitted:* Madoff case investigator

10   *His firm's account: MLSMK Investments Company v. JP Morgan Chase & Co., and JP Morgan Chase Bank, NA,* April 23, 2009

10   *had only $234 million: SIPC v. Bernard L. Madoff,* Stipulation and Order of Transfer of Funds by J.P. Morgan Chase Bank to Trustee, January 27, 2009

11   *The reports were prepared:* Eleanor Squillari

12   *Between 2006 and 2008: MLSMK Investments Company v. JP Morgan Chase & Co., and JP Morgan Chase Bank, NA,* April 23, 2009

13   *withdrew $5.5 million:* Massachusetts Secretary of State Complaint against Cohmad Securities Corporation, Exhibit 16, February 11, 2009

14   *Madoff flew to Palm Beach:* Madoff's 2008 calendar and Eleanor Squillari

14–15   *"too stretched":* Madoff case investigator

15   *Carl Shapiro agreed:* Person familiar with Shapiro's affairs

15   *November 19:* Madoff case investigator

16   *"hundreds of millions":* Source close to Wilpon

17   *The next day, Tuesday:* Ira Sorkin

18   *An hour or so earlier:* Eleanor Squillari

18   *ordered $10 million:* Massachusetts Secretary of State Complaint against Cohmad Securities Corporation, Exhibit 16, February 11, 2009

19   *brother, Peter, arrived first:* Eleanor Squillari

19   *because "he had recently made profits": USA v. Bernard L. Madoff,* Complaint, December 11, 2008

19   *"We have to meet with Dad"*: Person close to Mark and Andrew Madoff

20   *Peter stayed behind*: Eleanor Squillari

20   *Mark and Andy told the FBI*: Person close to Mark and Andrew Madoff

21   *Instead, his sons*: Person close to Mark and Andrew Madoff

CHAPTER TWO

23   *She told one family*: Sources close to Madoff family

24   *The two met as teenagers*: Sources close to Madoff family

25   *"tough guys"*: Jay Portnoy

26   *Bernie's parents*: Person familiar with Bernard Madoff

27   *"mislead"*: SEC Division of Enforcement Case Opening Report, January 4, 2006

27   *"evidence of fraud"*: SEC Division of Enforcement Case Closing Report, November 21, 2007

27   *Bernie went off to college*: University of Alabama records

27   *While he was away*: Sources close to Madoff family

27   *joining Sigma Alpha Mu*: University of Alabama 1957 yearbook

27   *"a fraternity of Jewish men"*: Sigma Alpha Mu Web site

27   *" for her own safety"*: University of Alabama Web site

28   *He enrolled at Hofstra*: Hofstra University records

28   *second lieutenant*: U.S. Army Reserve spokesperson

28   *She still found*: Sources close to Madoff family

28   *Fortunately for Hofstra*: Stuart Vincent, assistant VP for university relations at Hofstra University

29   *In early 1960*: FINRA Broker check records

29   *ran a suspect*: SEC News Digest, September 20, 1963

30   *In 1963, the SEC*: SEC News Digest, September 20, 1963

30   *in January 1964*: SEC News Digest, January 23, 1964

31   *Ruth and Bernie*: People who attended wedding

31   *Ruth breezed to a degree*: Queens College records

33   *Alpern's accounting office was*: Source familiar with the company

33   *The accountants guaranteed*: SEC News Digest, November 23, 1993

35   *The SEC imposed:* SEC News Digest, November 23, 1993

36   *A second set:* SEC News Digest, December 11, 1992; SEC News Digest, November 23, 1993

36   *They were not allowed:* Person familiar with the company

36   *and Mendelow insisted:* Stanley Arkin, lawyer for Steven Mendelow

38   *"Who was the broker":* Wall Street Journal, December 16, 1992

39   *When Ruth's father, Saul:* Saul Alpern's will

39   *After her husband's arrest:* SEC v. Madoff, Order on Consent, March 2, 2009

CHAPTER THREE

41   *It was late afternoon:* Interview Laurence Leamer, author, *Madness Under the Royal Palms*

42   *At Madoff's office:* Madoff employees

44   *Peter had seemed:* Madoff employees

46   *Calls were coming in:* Bernard Madoff's phone messages, December 11 and 12, 2008

47   *Some friends called:* Fax sent to Madoff from James Davin

48   *Carl Shapiro was at home:* Source close to Shapiro

48   *"Some late news":* CNN transcript, Anderson Cooper, December 11, 2008

51   *"to take care of the poor":* Person familiar with Madoff

53   *Similarly, Ruth didn't:* Sources close to Madoff family

55   *"Dear neighbors":* New York Times, January 12, 2009

55   *He ignored all requests:* Person familiar with Madoff

55   *"can't snap my picture":* Voice-mail message left for Nick Casale by Bernard Madoff

56   *One package contained:* USA v. Bernard L. Madoff, Letter from Marc Litt to Judge Ronald Ellis, January 6, 2009

56   *Bernie enclosed a note:* Person close to Mark and Andrew Madoff

56   *"sentimental personal items":* USA v. Bernard L. Madoff, Letter from Ira Sorkin to Judge Ronald L. Ellis, January 7, 2009

CHAPTER FOUR

60 *Ruth was at one point:* Madoff case investigator

61 *It was rare:* Madoff employees

62 *One of his first:* Amy Joel

64 *He became an investor:* USA v. Bernard L. Madoff, Government's Second Notice to Seek Forfeiture of Certain Assets, March 17, 2009

64 *requested the table up front:* Eleanor Squillari

64 *more than a trillion:* The Philoctetes Center for the Multidisciplinary Study of the Imagination, "The Future of the Stock Market," October 20, 2007

64 *"the world's largest market-maker":* Bernard L. Madoff Investment Securities LLC Web site

65 *"scores of leading securities firms":* Bernard L. Madoff Investment Securities LLC Web site

65 *At an industry:* The Philoctetes Center for the Multidisciplinary Study of the Imagination, "The Future of the Stock Market," October 20, 2007

67 *According to Madoff:* Bernard L. Madoff Investment Securities LLC Web site

70 *They both became multimillionaires:* Madoff case investigator

71 *$2 million home on:* Nassau County property records and Palm Beach County property records

71 *Her husband, Rudy:* NYC Department of Transportation spokesperson

71 *Investigators came to:* Madoff case investigator

73 *When questions were raised:* Massachusetts Secretary of State Complaint against Fairfield Greenwich Advisors LLC and Fairfield Greenwich (Bermuda) LTD, April 1, 2009

73 *Customers were told:* Massachusetts Secretary of State Complaint against Fairfield Greenwich Advisors LLC and Fairfield Greenwich (Bermuda) LTD, April 1, 2009

74 *One prominent investor:* Irving H. Picard v. Jeffry M. Picower et al., May 12, 2009

74 *Madoff said he made:* Massachusetts Secretary of State Complaint against Fairfield Greenwich Advisors LLC and Fairfield Greenwich (Bermuda) LTD, April 1, 2009

74 *he refused to answer:* Massachusetts Secretary of State Complaint against Fairfield Greenwich Advisors LLC and Fairfield Greenwich (Bermuda) LTD, April 1, 2009

74 *Then, on a regular basis:* Madoff case investigators said Madoff and DiPascali recorded the bogus trades once a month. Bernard Madoff told lawyer Joseph Cotchett that he and DiPascali recorded the trades "every other day."

74 *They often got sloppy: Irving H. Picard v. Fairfield Sentry Limited, Greenwich Sentry Limited L.P., and Greenwich Sentry Partners L.P.,* May 18, 2009

76 *"Frankie was wearing":* Madoff employee

77 *Madoff took cash draws: SIPC v. Bernard L. Madoff,* Affidavit of Michael Slattery, Jr., May 5, 2009

78 *Madoff used $2,225,000: SIPC v. Bernard L. Madoff,* Affidavit of Michael Slattery, Jr., Exhibits 16 and 17, May 5, 2009

81 *on one day in 1998: Irving H. Picard v. Fairfield Sentry Limited, Greenwich Sentry L.P., and Greenwich Sentry Partners, L.P.,* May 18, 2009

82 *Of the three, only one: Irving H. Picard v. Fairfield Sentry Limited, Greenwich Sentry Limited L.P., and Greenwich Sentry Partners L.P.,* May 18, 2009

84 *On the day after Christmas:* Surveillance photos, Milberg LLP

84 *more than $14 million: Securities and Exchange Commission v. David G. Friehling, Friehling & Horowitz, CPAs, P.C.,* March 18, 2009

CHAPTER FIVE

86 *But Ruth could:* Sources close to Madoff family

86 *"Was Ponzi Bernie Madoff":* New York *Daily News,* March 29, 2009

86 *Despite what the columnists':* Sources close to Madoff family

86 *Top Ten Signs Your Wife: Late Show with David Letterman,* March 30, 2009

86 *Sitting in the luxury Manhattan:* Sources close to Madoff family

88   *They traveled the world together:* Eleanor Squillari; *SIPC v. Bernard L. Madoff,* Affidavit of Michael Slattery, Jr., May 5, 2009; *SIPC v. Bernard L. Madoff,* Agreement by the Trustee and NetJet Sales, Inc., NetJets Aviation Inc., and NetJets Services, Inc., June 19, 2009

89   *Madoff was obsessive about:* Person familiar with Madoff family

91   *For the New York apartment:* Photographs obtained by ABC News

91   *Bernie arranged his suits:* Nick Casale

92   *The office summer party:* Madoff employees

93   *In the winter:* Madoff's 2006, 2007, and 2008 calendars

94   *The Madoffs first:* Madoff childhood friends

94   *Madoff paid $8 million:* Palm Beach property records

95   *Ruth Madoff often used: SIPC v. Bernard L. Madoff,* Exhibit 25, May 5, 2009

95   *Investigators discovered that: SIPC v. Bernard L. Madoff,* Exhibit 21, May 5, 2009

96   *They enjoyed each other's:* Sources close to Madoff family

98   *In January 2008, company: SIPC v. Bernard L. Madoff,* Exhibit 25, May 5, 2009

98   *had several billion dollars: MLSMK Investments Company v. JP Morgan Chase & Co. and JP Morgan Chase Bank, NA,* April 23, 2009

99   *Ruth and Bernie spent:* Sources close to Madoff family

100   *Her father steered him:* David Arenson and Cynthia Arenson

101   *received a master's degree:* New York University records

101   *Mostly, when Bernie:* Sources close to Madoff family

101   *Ruth emptied her accounts:* Massachusetts Secretary of State Complaint against Cohmad Securities Corporation, Exhibit 16, February 11, 2009.

CHAPTER SIX

103   *"Obviously, first of all":* Massachusetts Secretary of State complaint against Fairfield Greenwich Advisors LLC and Fairfield Greenwich (Bermuda) Ltd., Exhibit 1, April 1, 2009

104   *His scheme had narrowly:* Madoff case investigator

104 *Madoff's last close call:* SEC News Digest, November 30, 1992; *SEC News Digest,* December 11, 1992; *SEC News Digest,* November 23, 1993

105 *In 2004 the SEC initiated:* Sources familiar with the investigation

106 *Lawyers for Fairfield Greenwich:* Answer of Respondents, Fairfield Greenwich Advisors LLC and Fairfield Greenwich (Bermuda) Ltd., April 29, 2009, Massachusetts Securities Division, docket number 2009-0028

107 *Either FINRA or NASD: Picard v. Fairfield Sentry Limited, Greenwich Sentry, L.P., and Greenwich Sentry Partners, L.P.,* Complaint, May 18, 2009

107 *FINRA said it had no:* Testimony by Stephen Luparello, FINRA interim CEO, the Subcommittee on Capital Markets, Insurance, and Government Sponsored Enterprises, February 4, 2009

107 *At an industry conference:* The Philoctetes Center for the Multidisciplinary Study of the Imagination, "The Future of the Stock Market," October 20, 2007

108 *In 2000 Madoff was:* Former SEC chairman Arthur Levitt

110 *He supervised "the commission's":* BATS Newsletter, January 23, 2008

110 *Swanson was the SEC:* Source familiar with the investigation

111 *the separate SEC investigation:* SEC Division of Enforcement Case Opening Report, January 4, 2006

111 *Four months after:* Madoff family friend

112 *An employee: Mail on Sunday,* January 4, 2009

112 *came just two months:* SEC Division of Enforcement Case Closing Recommendation, November 21, 2007

112 *Madoff boasted about:* The Philoctetes Center for the Multidisciplinary Study of the Imagination, "The Future of the Stock Market," October 20, 2007

113 *The SEC inspector:* SEC official

115 *It turned into a full:* SEC Division of Enforcement Case Opening Report, January 4, 2006

115 *Markopolos became intrigued:* Harry Markopolos testimony, the U.S. House of Representatives Committee on Financial Services, February 4, 2009

116   *"Where did the missing":* Harry Markopolos testimony, the U.S. House of Representatives Committee on Financial Services, February 4, 2009

116   *Chelo even challenged:* Harry Markopolos testimony, the U.S. House of Representatives Committee on Financial Services, February 4, 2009

117   *At the SEC offices:* Source familiar with the investigation

118   *"voluntary production of":* SEC Division of Enforcement Case Opening Report, January 4, 2006

119   *Madoff then instructed:* Massachusetts Secretary of State Complaint against Fairfield Greenwich Advisors LLC and Fairfield Greenwich (Bermuda) Ltd., Exhibit 1, April 1, 2009

121   *There were six:* Madoff speaking to lawyer Joe Cotchett from Butner prison

121   *Madoff was asked: USA v. Bernard L. Madoff,* Information, March 10, 2009

121   *tens of billions:* Madoff case investigator

CHAPTER SEVEN

127   *who drank and partied hard:* Little Rick

129   *They talked about the blonde:* Little Rick

CHAPTER EIGHT

138   *Since 1989, he had:* Massachusetts Secretary of State Complaint against Fairfield Greenwich Advisors LLC and Fairfield Greenwich (Bermuda) Ltd., April 1, 2009

139   *His wife "shopped uptown Manhattan": Town & Country,* May 2005

140–141 *Merkin began investing: Irving H. Picard v. J. Ezra Merkin et al.,* May 6, 2009

141   *New York attorney general: The People of the State of New York, by Andrew Cuomo, Attorney General of the State of New York v. J. Ezra Merkin and Gabriel Capital Corporation,* April 6, 2009

141–142 *"Despite having clear indications": Irving H. Picard v. Stanley Chais et al.,* May 1, 2009

142   *Walter Noel was a:* Massachusetts Secretary of State

Complaint against Fairfield Greenwich Advisors LLC and Fairfield Greenwich (Bermuda) Ltd., April 1, 2009

142   *Noel and Tucker started by:* Massachusetts Secretary of State Complaint against Fairfield Greenwich Advisors LLC and Fairfield Greenwich (Bermuda) Ltd., April 1, 2009

144   *He claimed he made:* Ibid.

146   *Madoff had asked Tucker:* Ibid.

147   *Madoff had created:* Madoff case investigator

147   *"It had a logo":* Massachusetts Secretary of State Complaint against Fairfield Greenwich Advisors LLC and Fairfield Greenwich (Bermuda) Ltd., April 1, 2009

148   *able to honor some $3 billion:* Answer of Respondents, Fairfield Greenwich Advisors LLC and Fairfield Greenwich (Bermuda) Ltd., April 29, 2009, Massachusetts Securities Division, docket number 2009-0028

148   *Other than checking on:* Massachusetts Secretary of State Complaint against Fairfield Greenwich Advisors LLC and Fairfield Greenwich (Bermuda) Ltd., April 1, 2009

151   *Fairfield Greenwich tried to:* Ibid.

154   *Remarkably, Madoff told:* Ibid.

CHAPTER NINE

157   *was found dead:* NYC Police Department and NYC Medical Examiner's Office

158   *In the weeks before:* Madoff's 2008 calendar

158   *Harry Markopolos, apparently:* Harry Markopolos testimony, U.S. House of Representatives Committee on Financial Services, February 4, 2009

160   *totaled only 4,903:* Irving H. Picard

162   *One ninety-year-old:* Brad Friedman, Milberg LLP

163   *Madoff listed two:* Irving H. Picard v. Cohmad Securities Corporation et al., June 22, 2009

163–164   *"He cultivated an aura":* Securities and Exchange Commission v. Cohmad Securities Corporation, Maurice J. Cohn, Marcia B. Cohn, and Robert M. Jaffe, June 22, 2009

164   *Unbeknownst to many:* Ibid.

165   *Jaffe's payments from Madoff:* Ibid.

166 *With Jaffe's help:* Ibid.

168 *Sitting around the kitchen:* Sources close to Madoff family

168 *In an open letter: Newsweek*, December 23, 2008

172 *For example, one Madoff:* Irving H. Picard v. Jeffry M. Picower et al., May 12, 2009

174 *Investigators believe the "real":* Madoff case investigator

174 *Foxton was unaware:* Willard Foxton

CHAPTER TEN

177 *"We gave them everything":* Sources close to Madoff family

177 *Andy was crushed by his:* Source close to Madoff family

180 *payroll, at $163,500: SIPC v. Bernard L. Madoff,* Affidavit of Michael Slattery, Jr., May 5, 2009

181 *The bill would go: SIPC v. Bernard L. Madoff,* Exhibit 25, May 5, 2009

182 *In testimony before:* Massachusetts Secretary of State Complaint against Fairfield Greenwich Advisors LLC and Fairfield Greenwich (Bermuda) Ltd., April 1, 2009

184 *His employees in London:* Madoff case investigator

184 *In June, 2008, Mark again: SIPC v. Bernard L. Madoff,* Exhibits 13 and 14, May 5, 2009

185 *Andy buy a $4 million: SIPC v. Bernard L. Madoff,* Exhibits 11 and 12, May 5, 2009

188 *Peter was a major: SIPC v. Bernard L. Madoff,* Exhibit 4, May 5, 2009

188 *buy Peter a $237,600:* Joint Provisional Liquidators' Expedited Petition for Recognition of Foreign Proceeding and for Commencement of Chapter 15 Ancillary Case in Aid of Foreign Main Proceeding, April 14, 2009

188 *His wife, Marion, and daughter: SIPC v. Bernard L. Madoff,* Exhibit 25, May 5, 2009

190 *She later told people:* Madoff family friend

190 *The bankruptcy trustee charged:* Irving H. Picard v. Ruth Madoff, July 29, 2009

191 *"Actually it was my wife who":* The Philoctetes Center for the Multidisciplinary Study of the Imagination, "The Future of the Stock Market," October 20, 2007

192   *She charged dinners:* SIPC v. Bernard L. Madoff, Exhibit
       25, May 5, 2009

CHAPTER ELEVEN

197   *At one point, his sons:* Sources familiar with the investi-
       gation
201   *front for the illegal activity:* Madoff case investigator
203   *there could be a billion dollars:* Madoff case investigator
204   *Ike Sorkin called:* Sources close to Madoff family
204   *She was afraid:* Sources close to Madoff family
205   *She told people:* Sources close to Madoff family
205   *"magnet for celebrities":* Pierre Michel Salon Web site
206   *Within days of:* Sources close to Madoff family
206   *Ruth worried that:* Sources close to Madoff family
207   *Ruth continued:* Sources close to Madoff family
207   *The cleaning ladies:* SIPC v. Bernard L. Madoff, Affidavit of
       Michael Slattery, Jr., May 5, 2009
207   *As the news coverage:* Sources close to Madoff family
208   *Ruth remained estranged:* Sources close to Madoff family
208   *She knew the world:* Sources close to Madoff family
208   *While Ruth suffered for her:* Sources close to Madoff family

CHAPTER TWELVE

213   *Baroni had replaced Litt:* Madoff case investigator
214   *Conspicuous by her:* Sources close to Madoff family
214   *In an agreement with prosecutors:* USA v. Bernard L.
       Madoff, Stipulation and Order, June 26, 2009
217   *In a letter to the judge:* Letter to Judge Denny Chin from
       Ira Sorkin, June 22, 2009
218   *was about $13 billion:* USA v. Bernard L. Madoff, Govern-
       ment's Sentencing Memorandum, June 26, 2009
219   *than the initial $250,000:* Source familiar with the investi-
       gation
227   *She was denied permission:* Associated Press, July 3, 2009
228   *She was required: Irving H. Picard v. Ruth Madoff,* Stipu-
       lated Order, July 31, 2009

228   *who remains suspicious:* Madoff case investigator
228   *Ruth still loved Bernie and:* Sources close to Madoff family
229   *Even before she:* Sources close to Madoff family
229   *Ruth told people close:* Sources close to Madoff family
230   *"respected and trusted with":* Statement by Ruth Madoff,
       June 29, 2009

INDEX

GETTING
TO THE TRUTH.
THAT'S WHAT
HE DOES.

Brian Ross.
Chief Investigative Reporter.

abc NEWS

AMERICA'S #1 NEWS SOURCE